JEOPARDY!™

What Is Quiz Book 4?

Other Books

Jeopardy! . . . What Is Quiz Book 1?

Jeopardy! . . . What Is Quiz Book 2?

Jeopardy! . . . What Is Quiz Book 3?

JEOPARDY!™

What Is Quiz Book 4?

**Andrews McMeel
Publishing**

Kansas City

JEOPARDY!™

What Is Quiz Book 4?

**Andrews McMeel
Publishing**

Kansas City

JEOPARDY!

MIDDLE NAME LEE

IN 1998 THIS ACTRESS RETURNED TO THE SCREEN AS LAURIE STRODE IN "HALLOWEEN H2O"	$100	WHO IS
CODY & CASSIDY'S MOM	$200	WHO IS
SINCE LEAVING VAN HALEN, HE'S RELEASED SUCH SOLO ALBUMS AS "EAT 'EM & SMILE" & "SKYSCRAPER"	$300	WHO IS
HIS HIGH-PROFILE CLIENTS HAVE INCLUDED SAM SHEPPARD, PATTY HEARST & O.J. SIMPSON	$400	WHO IS
HE'S THE LEGENDARY SINGER & GUITARIST NICKNAMED "THE KING OF THE BOOGIE"	$500	WHO IS

JEOPARDY!

MIDDLE NAME LEE

$100 | WHO IS JAMIE LEE CURTIS? | **$100**

$200 | WHO IS KATHIE LEE GIFFORD? | **$200**

$300 | WHO IS DAVID LEE ROTH? | **$300**

$400 | WHO IS F. LEE BAILEY? | **$400**

$500 | WHO IS JOHN LEE HOOKER? | **$500**

JEOPARDY!

THE GLOBE

WITH OVER 50 INDE-PENDENT COUNTRIES, THIS CONTINENT HAS MORE THAN ANY OTHER	**$100**	WHAT IS
THE TYRRHENIAN SEA ON ITALY'S WEST COAST IS AN ARM OF THIS SEA	**$200**	WHAT IS
THE EQUATOR CROSSES MORE LAND IN THIS SOUTH AMERICAN NATION THAN ANY OTHER	**$300**	WHAT IS
THE SOUTHERN MIDSECTION OF THIS NATION IS KNOWN AS THE MASSIF CENTRAL	**$400**	WHAT IS
THIS COUNTRY'S NORTHERN BORDER TOUCHES CHINA, BHUTAN & NEPAL	**$500**	WHAT IS

JEOPARDY!

THE GLOBE

$100   WHAT IS AFRICA? $100

$200   WHAT IS THE MEDITERRANEAN? $200

$300   WHAT IS BRAZIL? $300

$400   WHAT IS FRANCE? $400

$500   WHAT IS INDIA? $500

JEOPARDY!

NATURE

A BEE DOES IT ABOUT 200 TIMES A SECOND; A MOSQUITO, 500 TIMES A SECOND	**$100**	WHAT IS
THE FLY AGARIC, A DEADLY TYPE OF THIS FUNGUS, WAS ONCE USED TO POISON FLIES	**$200**	WHAT IS
THIS KINGDOM IS COMMONLY DIVIDED INTO VASCULAR, IN-CLUDING CYCADS, & NONVASCULAR, IN-CLUDING HORNWORTS	**$300**	WHAT IS
THE WHELK, A CAR-NIVOROUS MARINE GASTROPOD, HAS A SHELL OF THIS SHAPE	**$400**	WHAT IS
IN A POPULAR SCIENCE EXPERIMENT IODINE ON A PIECE OF POTATO TURNS IT DARK, INDICATING THIS SUBSTANCE IS PRESENT	**$500**	WHAT IS

5

JEOPARDY!

NATURE

$100	WHAT IS BEAT ITS WINGS?	**$100**
$200	WHAT IS A MUSHROOM?	**$200**
$300	WHAT IS THE PLANT KINGDOM?	**$300**
$400	WHAT IS SPIRAL?	**$400**
$500	WHAT IS STARCH?	**$500**

JEOPARDY!™

PASTA BAR

PUTTANESCA IS A ZESTY SAUCE FEATURING CAPERS & THESE PIZZA FISHIES	$100	WHAT ARE
THE REGGIANO TYPE OF THIS HARD, DRY CHEESE IS ONE OF THE BEST FOR GRATING OVER PASTA	$200	WHAT IS
ORECCHIETTE ARE SHAPED LIKE THESE HUMAN ORGANS, BUT PEOPLE EAT THEM ANYWAY	$300	WHAT ARE
AGLIO E OLIO, ONE OF THE SIMPLEST SAUCES, MAINLY CONSISTS OF HEATED OLIVE OIL & THIS	$400	WHAT IS
THIS PASTA LOOKS KIND OF SQUIGGLY—APPROPRIATELY, SINCE ITS NAME MEANS "LITTLE WORMS"	$500	WHAT IS

JEOPARDY!

PASTA BAR

$100	**WHAT ARE ANCHOVIES?**	**$100**
$200	**WHAT IS PARMESAN?**	**$200**
$300	**WHAT ARE EARS?**	**$300**
$400	**WHAT IS GARLIC?**	**$400**
$500	**WHAT IS VERMICELLI?**	**$500**

JEOPARDY!

"RED", "WHITE" & "BLUE"

YOU'LL FIND IT AT 1600 PENNSYLVANIA AVENUE	**$100**	WHAT IS
WITH POLITICAL ASPIRATIONS, ELIZABETH DOLE RESIGNED AS HEAD OF THIS IN JANUARY 1999	**$200**	WHAT IS
WHEN WAVED IN THE AIR, IT'S A UNIVERSAL SIGN OF SURRENDER	**$300**	WHAT IS
IN 2000 THIS TEAM SIGNED DEION SANDERS	**$400**	WHAT IS
ACCESSIBLE ONLY BY BOAT, IT'S A NATURAL LIMESTONE CAVERN IN THE BAY OF NAPLES	**$500**	WHAT IS

JEOPARDY!

"RED", "WHITE" & "BLUE"

$100	WHAT IS THE WHITE HOUSE?	$100
$200	WHAT IS THE (AMERICAN) RED CROSS?	$200
$300	WHAT IS A WHITE FLAG?	$300
$400	WHAT IS THE WASHINGTON REDSKINS?	$400
$500	WHAT IS THE BLUE GROTTO?	$500

JEOPARDY!

CALAMITY JANE

JANE HAD SOME "DARK" TIMES AS A CAMP FOLLOWER OF AN EXPEDITION TO THESE SOUTH DAKOTA HILLS	**$100**	WHAT ARE
JANE'S JOB TITLE OF BULLWHACKER INDICATES SHE DROVE CATTLE WITH ONE OF THESE IMPLEMENTS	**$200**	WHAT IS
GENERAL GEORGE, WHOSE TROOPS JANE RODE WITH, HAD THIS LAST NAME THAT NIXON SAID DIDN'T APPLY TO HIM	**$300**	WHAT IS
A WOMAN SURFACED IN 1941 CLAIMING TO BE THE DAUGHTER OF JANE & THIS MAN WHO PLAYED ONE POKER HAND TOO MANY	**$400**	WHO IS
JANE'S GIG AT THE 1901 PAN-AMERICAN EXPO IN THIS CITY WAS OVERSHADOWED BY THE McKINLEY ASSASSINATION THERE	**$500**	WHAT IS

11

JEOPARDY!

CALAMITY JANE

$100	WHAT ARE THE BLACK HILLS?	**$100**
$200	WHAT IS A (BULL)WHIP?	**$200**
$300	WHAT IS CROOK?	**$300**
$400	WHO IS WILD BILL HICKOK?	**$400**
$500	WHAT IS BUFFALO?	**$500**

DOUBLE JEOPARDY!

ANCIENT ANIMALS

BEFORE THIS ANIMAL BECAME COMMON, ROMANS USED THE FERRET FOR VERMIN CONTROL	**$200**	WHAT IS
HERODOTUS TOLD THE TALE OF ARION'S RESCUE AT SEA BY ONE OF THESE MAMMALS	**$400**	WHAT IS
A JAPANESE FOLKTALE TELLS OF URASHIMA TARO WHO SAVES ONE OF THESE SEA REPTILES THAT TURNS INTO A YOUNG WOMAN	**$600**	WHAT IS
THESE ANIMALS WERE INVOLVED IN THE PREMIERE EVENT IN THE FUNERAL GAMES FOR PATROCLUS	**$800**	WHAT ARE
THE "LUCANIAN COWS" PYRRHUS USED IN HIS INVASION OF ITALY WERE THESE, FROM ASIA	**$1000**	WHAT ARE

DOUBLE JEOPARDY!

ANCIENT ANIMALS

$200	WHAT IS THE CAT?	$200
$400	WHAT IS A DOLPHIN?	$400
$600	WHAT IS A TURTLE?	$600
$800	WHAT ARE HORSES?	$800
$1000	WHAT ARE ELEPHANTS?	$1000

DOUBLE JEOPARDY!

COLLEGES

IRVIN FELD FOUNDED A COLLEGE IN VENICE, FLORIDA IN 1968 TO TRAIN THESE PERFORMERS FOR THE CIRCUS	$200	WHAT ARE
MESA STATE IS A COLLEGE IN GRAND JUNCTION IN THIS STATE	$400	WHAT IS
A COLLEGE OF PODIATRY IN CHICAGO IS NAMED FOR THIS DOCTOR	$600	WHO IS
THE GRADUATES OF THIS OWATONNA, MINNESOTA BAPTIST BIBLE COLLEGE MUST BE POPPIN' FRESH (WE COULDN'T RESIST THE JOKE)	$800	WHAT IS
LOCATED IN CHARLESTON, IT'S "THE MILITARY COLLEGE OF SOUTH CAROLINA"	$1000	WHAT IS

DOUBLE JEOPARDY!

COLLEGES

$200	WHAT ARE CLOWNS?	**$200**
$400	WHAT IS COLORADO?	**$400**
$600	WHO IS DR. WILLIAM M. SCHOLL?	**$600**
$800	WHAT IS PILLSBURY (BAPTIST BIBLE COLLEGE)?	**$800**
$1000	WHAT IS THE CITADEL?	**$1000**

DOUBLE JEOPARDY!

ON CD

ON THE COVER OF THIS DUO'S BOXED SET "OLD FRIENDS", A CIGARETTE HAS BEEN AIRBRUSHED OUT OF PAUL'S FINGERS	**$200**	WHO ARE
MADONNA TOLD THESE "STORIES" ON A 1994 CD	**$400**	WHAT ARE
"THE REAL SLIM SHADY" APPEARS ON THE CD OF THIS RAPPER'S "MARSHALL MATHERS LP"	**$600**	WHO IS
THIS NIRVANA CD TITLE IS FOUND IN THE LYRICS OF "SMELLS LIKE TEEN SPIRIT"	**$800**	WHAT IS
"PERSONAL JESUS" & "ENJOY THE SILENCE" ARE ON A 1998 COMPILATION BY THIS ENGLISH BAND WITH A FRENCH NAME	**$1000**	WHAT IS

DOUBLE JEOPARDY!

ON CD

$200	WHO ARE SIMON & GARFUNKEL?	$200
$400	WHAT ARE BEDTIME STORIES?	$400
$600	WHO IS EMINEM?	$600
$800	WHAT IS "NEVERMIND"?	$800
$1000	WHAT IS DEPECHE MODE?	$1000

DOUBLE JEOPARDY!

LITERATURE

A 1927 BOOK OF SHORT STORIES BY ERNEST HEMINGWAY WAS TITLED "MEN WITHOUT" THESE	**$200**	WHAT ARE
POET WHO WROTE, "BEFORE I BUILT A WALL I'D ASK TO KNOW WHAT I WAS WALLING IN OR WALLING OUT"	**$400**	WHO IS
IN JAMES FENIMORE COOPER'S "THE PIO-NEERS" OLIVER EDWARDS IS THIS "NATTY" FRONTIERS-MAN'S COMPANION	**$600**	WHO IS
THE FATHER OF THIS "GOOD-BYE, MR. CHIPS" AUTHOR WAS A SCHOOLTEACHER, NOT A HOTELIER	**$800**	WHO IS
BALZAC WROTE "LA COMEDIE HUMAINE" IN THE 1840s & THIS AMERICAN WROTE "THE HUMAN COM-EDY" IN THE 1940s	**$1000**	WHO IS

DOUBLE JEOPARDY!

LITERATURE

$200   WHAT ARE "WOMEN"? $200

$400   WHO IS ROBERT FROST? $400

$600   WHO IS NATTY BUMPPO? $600

$800   WHO IS JAMES HILTON? $800

$1000   WHO IS WILLIAM SAROYAN? $1000

DOUBLE JEOPARDY!

AIRPORT PEOPLE

AN ORANGE COUNTY, CALIFORNIA AIRPORT IS NAMED FOR THIS "DUKE" OF THE MOVIES	**$200**	WHO IS
THIS MAN FOR WHOM A BUSY MIDWESTERN AIRPORT IS NAMED WAS A WWII FLYING HERO	**$400**	WHO IS
WASHINGTON, D.C. HAS AN AIRPORT NAMED FOR THIS '50s SECRETARY OF STATE	**$600**	WI IO IS
THE NAME OF THIS RENAISSANCE PAINTER/SCULPTOR/ ARCHITECT/BOTANIST/ MATHEMATICIAN IS ON ROME'S AIRPORT	**$800**	WHO IS
IT'S THE NEW YORK CITY AIRPORT NAMED FOR A FORMER NEW YORK CITY MAYOR	**$1000**	WHAT IS

DOUBLE JEOPARDY!

AIRPORT PEOPLE

$200	WHO IS JOHN WAYNE?	$200
$400	WHO IS EDWARD "BUTCH" O'HARE?	$400
$600	WHO IS JOHN FOSTER DULLES?	$600
$800	WHO IS LEONARDO DA VINCI?	$800
$1000	WHAT IS LaGUARDIA?	$1000

DOUBLE JEOPARDY!

QUASI-RELATED PAIRS

A MIXED FRUIT JUICE BEVERAGE & MISS GARLAND	**$200**	WHAT IS
THE SINGER OF "RING OF FIRE" & THE STAR OF "ME, MYSELF & IRENE"	**$400**	WHO ARE
AN ETHNIC GROUP OF NORTHERN IRAQ & A TYPE OF HIGHWAY "STATION" FOR TRUCKERS	**$600**	WHAT ARE
AN ENGLISH EMPIRICAL PHILOSOPHER & THE AUTHOR OF "THE STAR-SPANGLED BANNER"	**$800**	WHO ARE
SLANG TERM FOR A GUY FROM SYDNEY & THE VETERINARIAN AUTHOR OF "ALL CREATURES GREAT AND SMALL"	**$1000**	WHO ARE

DOUBLE JEOPARDY!

QUASI-RELATED PAIRS

$200	WHAT IS PUNCH & JUDY?	$200
$400	WHO ARE CASH & CARREY?	$400
$600	WHAT ARE KURDS & WEIGH?	$600
$800	WHO ARE LOCKE AND KEY?	$800
$1000	WHO ARE AUSSIE & HERRIOT?	$1000

BASKETBALL

2 OF THE 3 NBA TEAMS
WHOSE NAMES DON'T
END WITH THE LETTER S

WHAT ARE

FINAL JEOPARDY!

BASKETBALL

WHAT ARE THE
MIAMI HEAT,
ORLANDO MAGIC
& UTAH JAZZ?

JEOPARDY!

DID THEY MOVE IT?

STUTTGART IS A LITTLE WAYS FROM LITTLE ROCK IN THIS STATE	**$100**	WHAT IS
YOU'LL FIND LAKE GENEVA IF YOU HEAD DUE WEST FROM KENOSHA IN THIS STATE	**$200**	WHAT IS
AS WELL AS IN CALIFORNIA, THERE'S A LOS ANGELES ABOUT 200 MILES SOUTH OF SANTIAGO IN THIS COUNTRY	**$300**	WHAT IS
IT MAKES SENSE THAT INVERNESS IS IN THIS CANADIAN ATLANTIC PROVINCE	**$400**	WHAT IS
YOU'LL FIND A BUENOS AIRES IN THIS COUNTRY THAT'S JUST NORTH OF PANAMA	**$500**	WHAT IS

JEOPARDY!

DID THEY MOVE IT?

$100	WHAT IS ARKANSAS?	$100
$200	WHAT IS WISCONSIN?	$200
$300	WHAT IS CHILE?	$300
$400	WHAT IS NOVA SCOTIA?	$400
$500	WHAT IS COSTA RICA?	$500

JEOPARDY!™

I HEARD THE "NEWS"

CANINE TERM FOR AN INQUISITIVE REPORTER	**$100**	WHAT IS
THESE SHORT FILMS OF CURRENT EVENTS, SUCH AS "THE MARCH OF TIME" SERIES, PLAYED IN MOVIE HOUSES IN THE '40s	**$200**	WHAT ARE
IN 2000 IT HAD CONSECUTIVE COVERS ON SUPREME COURT CONTROVERSIES & HARRY POTTER	**$300**	WHAT IS
IT'S THE INEXPENSIVE PAPER MADE FROM WOOD PULP OF WHICH YOUR MORNING PAPER IS MADE	**$400**	WHAT IS
THIS RUPERT MURDOCH COMPANY OWNS THE L.A. DODGERS, THE NEW YORK POST & FOX STUDIOS	**$500**	WHAT IS

JEOPARDY!

I HEARD THE "NEWS"

$100	WHAT IS NEWSHOUND?	$100
$200	WHAT ARE NEWSREELS?	$200
$300	WHAT IS "NEWSWEEK"?	$300
$400	WHAT IS NEWSPRINT?	$400
$500	WHAT IS NEWS CORPORATION?	$500

JEOPARDY!

U.S. HISTORY

RADICAL REPUBLICANS IMPEACHED & TRIED TO REMOVE THIS PRESIDENT IN 1868	$100	WHO IS
THIS AVUNCULAR NICKNAME FOR THE GOVERNMENT WAS COINED BY THOSE AGAINST THE WAR OF 1812	$200	WHAT IS
WHEN EAST & WEST WERE LINKED BY THIS IN OCTOBER 1861, THE DAYS OF THE PONY EXPRESS WERE NUMBERED	$300	WHAT IS
IN 1851 STONEWALL JACKSON BECAME AN INSTRUCTOR AT VMI, THIS SCHOOL	$400	WHAT IS
THIS SECRETARY OF STATE RETIRED IN 1869, 2 YEARS AFTER HIS "FOLLY"	$500	WHO IS

JEOPARDY!

U.S. HISTORY

$100	WHO IS ANDREW JOHNSON?	**$100**
$200	WHAT IS UNCLE SAM?	**$200**
$300	WHAT IS THE TELEGRAPH?	**$300**
$400	WHAT IS THE VIRGINIA MILITARY INSTITUTE?	**$400**
$500	WHO IS WILLIAM SEWARD?	**$500**

JEOPARDY!

PALINDROMIC WORDS

WHEN MALES TAKE ON FEMALES, IT'S CALLED "THE BATTLE OF" THESE	$100	WHAT ARE
AIR TRAFFIC CONTROLLERS CHECK THIS SCREEN TO GET THE DISH ON THE FLIGHT PATH OF A PLANE	$200	WHAT IS
A CARPENTER'S TOOL, OR THE TYPE OF "HEAD" A SENSIBLE PERSON HAS	$300	WHAT IS
THIS ESKIMO CANOE IS STEERED WITH A DOUBLE-BLADED PADDLE	$400	WHAT IS
MAJOR LEAGUE PITCHERS DREAD INJURY TO THIS "CUFF"	$500	WHAT IS

JEOPARDY!

PALINDROMIC WORDS

$100 — WHAT ARE THE SEXES? — $100

$200 — WHAT IS RADAR? — $200

$300 — WHAT IS LEVEL? — $300

$400 — WHAT IS A KAYAK? — $400

$500 — WHAT IS ROTATOR? — $500

JEOPARDY!

CRITTERS

THIS BEAR, URSUS MARITIMUS, SPENDS MUCH OF ITS TIME ON ICE FLOES & MAY BEAR ITS YOUNG ON THEM	**$100**	WHAT IS
THE RUBY-THROATED SPECIES OF THIS BIRD USUALLY LAYS 2 TINY EGGS ABOUT THE SIZE OF NAVY BEANS	**$200**	WHAT IS
GORILLAS RARELY WALK UPRIGHT, BUT USUALLY SUPPORT THEIR UPPER BODIES BY WALKING ON THESE HAND PARTS	**$300**	WHAT ARE
THIS ARMORED MAMMAL IS ONE OF THE FEW KNOWN ANIMAL HOSTS FOR THE BACTERIUM THAT CAUSES LEPROSY IN HUMANS	**$400**	WHAT IS
THE LARGEST TYPE OF THIS TAILED AMPHIBIAN IN THE U.S. IS THE HELLBENDER, WHICH MAY REACH 3 FEET	**$500**	WHAT IS

JEOPARDY!

CRITTERS

$100	WHAT IS THE POLAR BEAR?	$100
$200	WHAT IS THE HUMMINGBIRD?	$200
$300	WHAT ARE KNUCKLES?	$300
$400	WHAT IS THE ARMADILLO?	$400
$500	WHAT IS THE SALAMANDER?	$500

JEOPARDY!

PEOPLE

IN THE '60s HIS TRADEMARKS WERE JEWELED COSTUMES & ELABORATELY DESIGNED PIANOS TOPPED BY CANDELABRA	**$100**	WHO IS
IN 1998 SUPERMODEL REBECCA ROMIJN MARRIED THIS FORMER STAR OF TV's "FULL HOUSE"	**$200**	WHO IS
IN 2000 THIS WOMAN WHO WANTED TO MARRY A MULTI-MILLIONAIRE TOOK IT OFF FOR PLAYBOY MAGAZINE	**$300**	WHO IS
THIS "FAST CAR" SINGER HONED HER STYLE ON THE BOSTON CIRCUIT WHILE A STUDENT AT TUFTS UNIVERSITY	**$400**	WHO IS
SOMEDAY, THIS YOUNGER BROTHER OF PRINCE WILLIAM MIGHT WANT TO FORGET HIS DAYS AS A SPICE GIRLS FAN	**$500**	WHO IS

JEOPARDY!

PEOPLE

$100	WHO IS LIBERACE?	**$100**
$200	WHO IS JOHN STAMOS?	**$200**
$300	WHO IS DARVA CONGER?	**$300**
$400	WHO IS TRACY CHAPMAN?	**$400**
$500	WHO IS PRINCE HARRY?	**$500**

DOUBLE JEOPARDY!

RUSSIAN "T" ROOM

HIS WRITING CAREER BEGAN WITH THE SHORT NOVEL "DETSTVO" IN 1852; THE MUCH LONGER PIECES CAME LATER	**$200**	WHO IS
THE TAIGA IS THE FOREST LAND OF RUSSIA & THIS IS ITS NEARLY TREELESS NORTHERN BELT	**$400**	WHAT IS
IN 1919 HE & LENIN FOUNDED THE THIRD INTERNATIONAL TO BRING TOGETHER COMRADES FROM AROUND THE WORLD	**$600**	WHO IS
A GROUP OF 3 IN POWER, OR A VEHICLE DRAWN BY 3 HORSES ABREAST	**$800**	WHAT IS
IN 1992 THIS NEWS AGENCY ADDED ITAR TO ITS NAME, FOR THE INFORMATION-TELEGRAPH AGENCY OF RUSSIA	**$1000**	WHAT IS

DOUBLE JEOPARDY!

RUSSIAN "T" ROOM

$200	WHO IS LEO TOLSTOY?	$200
$400	WHAT IS THE TUNDRA?	$400
$600	WHO IS LEON TROTSKY?	$600
$800	WHAT IS A TROIKA?	$800
$1000	WHAT IS TASS?	$1000

DOUBLE JEOPARDY!

THE ARTISTIC TOUCH

THIS ART PRACTICED BY WILLIAM BLAKE PRECEDES "PRINTING" IN THE NAME OF A U.S. BUREAU	**$200**	WHAT IS
TO FILM JACKSON POLLOCK AT WORK, YOU'D SAY "LIGHTS! CAMERA!" THIS TYPE OF PAINTING	**$400**	WHAT IS
IN THE 1880s THIS ARTIST WITH "NOIR" IN HIS NAME BROKE WITH IMPRESSIONISM & BEGAN USING MORE BLACK	**$600**	WHO IS
THE INITIALS OF THIS BRITISH SEASCAPE WHIZ STOOD FOR JOSEPH MALLORD WILLIAM	**$800**	WHO IS
LAST NAME OF FORMER HUSBAND & WIFE WALTER & MARGARET, KNOWN FOR PAINTING LARGE-EYED WAIFS	**$1000**	WHAT IS

DOUBLE JEOPARDY!

THE ARTISTIC TOUCH

$200 — WHAT IS ENGRAVING? — $200

$400 — WHAT IS ACTION PAINTING? — $400

$600 — WHO IS PIERRE-AUGUSTE RENOIR? — $600

$800 — WHO IS J.M.W. TURNER? — $800

$1000 — WHAT IS KEANE? — $1000

DOUBLE JEOPARDY!

FLYING

IN HIS FIRST STORIES, HE WAS ABLE TO "LEAP TALL BUILDINGS AT A SINGLE BOUND"; HE DIDN'T FLY UNTIL LATER	**$200**	WHO IS
A FLAT ONE NEEDS A TAIL TO SUPPLY DRAG & TO KEEP IT POINTED TO THE SKY	**$400**	WHAT IS
"HE FLIES THROUGH THE AIR WITH THE GREATEST OF EASE", THE DARING YOUNG MAN ON THIS APPARATUS	**$600**	WHAT IS
THIS "ARCTIC" BIRD, STERNA PARADISAEA, BREEDS ON THE COASTS OF NORTH AMERICA BUT MAKES ITS WINTER HOME IN THE ANTARCTIC	**$800**	WHAT IS
ON NOV. 20, 1953, IN A DOUGLAS D-558-2, SCOTT CROSSFIELD FIRST REACHED THIS SPEED	**$1000**	WHAT IS

DOUBLE JEOPARDY!

FLYING

WHO IS SUPERMAN?

$200 $200

WHAT IS A KITE?

$400 $400

WHAT IS THE FLYING TRAPEZE?

$600 $600

WHAT IS THE ARCTIC TERN?

$800 $800

WHAT IS MACH 2?

$1000 $1000

DOUBLE JEOPARDY!

NEXT IN LINE, PLEASE

YEAR, DECADE, CENTURY ...	**$200**	WHAT IS
TAFT, WILSON, HARDING ...	**$400**	WHO IS
IOTA, KAPPA, LAMBDA ...	**$600**	WHAT IS
TENDERFOOT, SECOND CLASS, FIRST CLASS ...	**$800**	WHAT IS
PENNSYLVANIAN PERIOD, PERMIAN PERIOD, TRIASSIC PERIOD ...	**$1000**	WHAT IS

DOUBLE JEOPARDY!

NEXT IN LINE, PLEASE

$200	WHAT IS MILLENNIUM?	**$200**
$400	WHO IS (CALVIN) COOLIDGE?	**$400**
$600	WHAT IS MU?	**$600**
$800	WHAT IS STAR (SCOUT)?	**$800**
$1000	WHAT IS THE JURASSIC PERIOD?	**$1000**

DOUBLE JEOPARDY!

THE CINEMA

THIS BEATLE NOT ONLY STARRED IN "GIVE MY REGARDS TO BROAD STREET", HE WROTE THE SCREENPLAY & THE SCORE	**$200**	WHO IS
ADS FOR THIS 2000 HORROR SPOOF READ, "NO MERCY. NO SHAME. NO SEQUEL."	**$400**	WHAT IS
"TITANIC" TIED THIS 1959 FILM'S RECORD OF 11 OSCARS BUT DIDN'T OVERTAKE IT	**$600**	WHAT IS
AS A CHILD, THIS "DOCTOR ZHIVAGO" CO-STAR HAD A BIT ROLE IN HER FATHER'S FILM "LIMELIGHT"	**$800**	WHO IS
WE DON'T KNOW WHICH EXECUTIVE "GREEN-LIT" THIS 1999 FILM STARRING SARAH POLLEY & SCOTT WOLF	**$1000**	WHAT IS

DOUBLE JEOPARDY!

THE CINEMA

$200	WHO IS PAUL McCARTNEY?	$200
$400	WHAT IS "SCARY MOVIE"?	$400
$600	WHAT IS "BEN-HUR"?	$600
$800	WHO IS GERALDINE CHAPLIN?	$800
$1000	WHAT IS "GO"?	$1000

48

DOUBLE JEOPARDY!

POE FOLKS

Clue	Value	Response
"I WAS A CHILD AND SHE WAS A CHILD, IN THIS KINGDOM BY THE SEA, BUT WE LOVED WITH A LOVE THAT WAS MORE THAN LOVE, I" & SHE	$200	WHO IS
LAST NAME OF RODERICK & HIS SISTER MADELINE, WHO FALL DEAD JUST BEFORE THEIR HOUSE FALLS INTO A MOUNTAIN LAKE	$400	WHAT IS
THIS MASKED APPARITION JOINS PRINCE PROSPERO & HIS FRIENDS AT A COSTUME BALL IN A SECLUDED CASTLE	$600	WHAT IS
THIS SCHOLARLY AMATEUR DETECTIVE SOLVES THE BAFFLING CASE OF "THE PURLOINED LETTER"	$800	WHO IS
HIS "NARRATIVE" RECOUNTS HIS ADVENTURES ON THE GRAMPUS AS IT SAILS FROM NANTUCKET TO THE SOUTH SEAS	$1000	WHO IS

DOUBLE JEOPARDY!

POE FOLKS

$200   WHO IS ANNABEL LEE? $200

$400   WHAT IS USHER? $400

$600   WHAT IS THE RED DEATH? $600

$800   WHO IS C. AUGUSTE DUPIN? $800

$1000   WHO IS A. GORDON PYM? $1000

FINAL JEOPARDY!

'90s TRENDS

THIS ADORNMENT
WAS SEEN ON CHER,
DENNIS RODMAN &
THE 5,000-YEAR-OLD
"ICEMAN" FOUND IN 1991

WHAT IS

FINAL JEOPARDY!

'90s TRENDS

WHAT IS A TATTOO?

JEOPARDY!

FLAGS

THIS CANADIAN PROVINCE'S FLAG SHOWS THE SETTING SUN & WAVY BLUE BARS REPRESENTING THE PACIFIC OCEAN	**$100**	WHAT IS
FRANCE'S TRICOLOR FLAG FEATURES RED & BLUE—THE COLORS OF PARIS—& THIS, THE ROYAL COLOR OF THE BOURBON KINGS	**$200**	WHAT IS
FLAG FANS MISS THE WACKED-OUT OIL-WELL-IN-THE-MOUN-TAINS PICTURE ON THIS EUROPEAN FLAG IN ITS COMMUNIST DAYS	**$300**	WHAT IS
THIS STATE'S FLAG FEATURES A MOTHER PELICAN WITH ITS YOUNG	**$400**	WHAT IS
THE STAFF & HAT OF THE BISHOP OF URGEL CAN BE FOUND ON THIS TINY PYRENEES COUNTRY'S FLAG	**$500**	WHAT IS

JEOPARDY!

FLAGS

$100	WHAT IS BRITISH COLUMBIA?	**$100**
$200	WHAT IS WHITE?	**$200**
$300	WHAT IS ROMANIA?	**$300**
$400	WHAT IS LOUISIANA?	**$400**
$500	WHAT IS ANDORRA?	**$500**

JEOPARDY!

GORDONS

Clue	Value	Response
BEFORE HE WAS THE LEAD SINGER OF THE POLICE, HE WAS A TEACHER NAMED GORDON SUMNER	$100	WHO IS
THIS BRAWNY FICTIONAL SPACE HERO WAS A YALE GRADUATE & A WORLD-CLASS POLO PLAYER	$200	WHO IS
DJ VENUS FLYTRAP WAS THE ALTER EGO OF GORDON SIMS ON THIS SITCOM	$300	WHAT IS
HIS HIT SONGS INCLUDE "SUNDOWN" & "THE WRECK OF THE EDMUND FITZGERALD"	$400	WHO IS
IN APRIL 1977 JIMMY CARTER COMMUTED HIS SENTENCE TO 8 YEARS, ALLOWING HIM TO BE PAROLED LATER THAT YEAR	$500	WHO IS

JEOPARDY!™

GORDONS

$100	WHO IS STING?	**$100**
$200	WHO IS FLASH GORDON?	**$200**
$300	WHAT IS "WKRP IN CINCINNATI"?	**$300**
$400	WHO IS GORDON LIGHTFOOT?	**$400**
$500	WHO IS G. GORDON LIDDY?	**$500**

JEOPARDY!

LITHUANIAN HISTORY

EVEN WITHOUT A PROCLAMATION FROM LINCOLN, MANY LITHUANIAN SERFS WERE GIVEN THIS AROUND 1861	$100	WHAT IS
LITHUANIA & THESE 2 OTHER BALTIC REPUBLICS LEFT THE SOVIET UNION IN 1991	$200	WHAT ARE
IN THE 1860s A RUSSIFICATION PROGRAM MEANT LITHUANIAN BOOKS HAD TO USE THIS RUSSIAN ALPHABET	$300	WHAT IS
"TAUTISKA GIESME", WRITTEN IN THE 19th CENTURY BY VINCAS KUDIRKA, BECAME THIS NATIONAL SYMBOL	$400	WHAT IS
AN "EARLY" NATIONALIST NEWS-PAPER WAS CALLED AUSRA, MEANING THIS TIME OF DAY	$500	WHAT IS

JEOPARDY!

LITHUANIAN HISTORY

$100   WHAT IS EMANCIPATION? $100

$200   WHAT ARE ESTONIA & LATVIA? $200

$300   WHAT IS THE CYRILLIC ALPHABET? $300

$400   WHAT IS THE LITHUANIAN NATIONAL ANTHEM? $400

$500   WHAT IS DAWN? $500

JEOPARDY!™

DEMOCRATS

THIS FORMER HOOPS STAR CHALLENGED AL GORE FOR THE 2000 DEMOCRATIC NOMINATION	**$100**	WHO IS
IN 1998 JOHN CONYERS WAS REELECTED WITH 87% OF THE VOTE IN THIS STATE'S 14th CONGRESSIONAL DISTRICT	**$200**	WHAT IS
HE DIDN'T OFFICIALLY MEET WITH HIS CABINET FOR THE FIRST 2 YEARS OF HIS TERM, PREFERRING HIS "KITCHEN CABINET"	**$300**	WHO IS
IN 1998 TOM HARKIN & THIS TOM, THE SENATE'S DEMOCRATIC LEADER, CHAIRED A HEARING ON HOG PRICES	**$400**	WHO IS
THIS DEMOCRAT'S "CROSS OF GOLD" SPEECH SUPPORTED THE BIMETALLIC THEORY	**$500**	WHO IS

JEOPARDY!

DEMOCRATS

$100	WHO IS BILL BRADLEY?	**$100**
$200	WHAT IS MICHIGAN?	**$200**
$300	WHO IS ANDREW JACKSON?	**$300**
$400	WHO IS TOM DASCHLE?	**$400**
$500	WHO IS WILLIAM JENNINGS BRYAN?	**$500**

JEOPARDY!

LOGO LADIES

THIS MINNESOTA-BASED BUTTER MAKER USES AN INDIAN MAIDEN AS ITS TRADEMARK	**$100**	WHAT IS
BILLBOARDS FOR "LITTLE MISS" THIS SUNTAN LOTION BECAME MIAMI LANDMARKS IN THE '50s	**$200**	WHAT IS
IN 1915 LORRAINE COLLETT OF FRESNO BECAME THE ORIGINAL MODEL FOR THIS BRAND OF RAISINS	**$300**	WHAT IS
THE SYMBOL OF THIS MOVIE COMPANY FOUNDED BY HARRY COHN GOT A MAKE-OVER IN 1993	**$400**	WHAT IS
DEBRA McKEE, FOR WHOM THESE SNACK CAKES WERE NAMED, GREW UP TO BE A DIRECTOR OF THE COMPANY THAT MAKES THEM	**$500**	WHAT ARE

JEOPARDY!

LOGO LADIES

$100	WHAT IS LAND O'LAKES?	**$100**
$200	WHAT IS COPPERTONE?	**$200**
$300	WHAT IS SUN-MAID?	**$300**
$400	WHAT IS COLUMBIA PICTURES?	**$400**
$500	WHAT ARE LITTLE DEBBIE (SNACK CAKES)?	**$500**

JEOPARDY!

"BAG" 'EM UP

IT'S WHERE TIGER CAN KEEP HIS IRONS & DRIVERS & TEES, OH MY!	**$100**	WHAT IS
BELLOWING HIGHLAND INSTRUMENT	**$200**	WHAT ARE
IT'S A MIDDLE EAST CAPITAL	**$300**	WHAT IS
DERIVED FROM THE ITALIAN FOR "LITTLE STICK", IT'S A LONG, NARROW LOAF OF FRENCH BREAD	**$400**	WHAT IS
A TRIFLE, OR A SHORT PIECE OF MUSIC	**$500**	WHAT IS

JEOPARDY!™

"BAG" 'EM UP

$100	WHAT IS A GOLF BAG?	$100
$200	WHAT ARE THE BAGPIPES?	$200
$300	WHAT IS BAGHDAD?	$300
$400	WHAT IS A BAGUETTE?	$400
$500	WHAT IS A BAGATELLE?	$500

DOUBLE JEOPARDY!

QUOTABLE DEFINITIONS

JOHN MASON BROWN'S FAMOUS DEFINITION OF THIS IS "CHEWING GUM FOR THE EYES"	**$200**	WHAT IS
HISTORIAN BRUCE CATTON CALLED THIS SPORT "THE GREATEST CONVERSATION PIECE EVER INVENTED IN AMERICA"	**$400**	WHAT IS
SAMUEL JOHNSON DEFINED THIS SENTIMENT AS "THE LAST REFUGE OF A SCOUNDREL"	**$600**	WHAT IS
AUTHOR WHO DEFINED A CLASSIC AS "A BOOK WHICH PEOPLE PRAISE AND DON'T READ"	**$800**	WHO IS
SHAKESPEARE WROTE IT "IS A PIPE BLOWN BY SURMISES, JEALOUSIES, CONJECTURES"; BUT THAT'S JUST WHAT HE HEARD	**$1000**	WHAT IS

DOUBLE JEOPARDY!

QUOTABLE DEFINITIONS

$200	WHAT IS TELEVISION?	$200
$400	WHAT IS BASEBALL?	$400
$600	WHAT IS PATRIOTISM?	$600
$800	WHO IS MARK TWAIN?	$800
$1000	WHAT IS RUMOR?	$1000

DOUBLE JEOPARDY!

NORTH DAKOTA

Clue	Value	Response
THE STATE CAPITOL IN THIS CITY IS SOMETIMES CALLED "THE SKYSCRAPER OF THE PRAIRIE"	$200	WHAT IS
NORTH DAKOTA BECAME A STATE ON NOVEMBER 2, 1889, THE SAME DAY AS THIS OTHER STATE	$400	WHAT IS
SHE JOINED THE LEWIS & CLARK EXPEDITION IN WHAT IS NOW NORTH DAKOTA	$600	WHO IS
HE SAID, "I WOULD NEVER HAVE BEEN PRESIDENT IF IT HAD NOT BEEN FOR MY EXPERIENCES IN NORTH DAKOTA"	$800	WHO IS
THE AUTHOR OF "HONDO" & OTHER WESTERNS, HE WAS BORN IN JAMESTOWN, NORTH DAKOTA	$1000	WHO IS

DOUBLE JEOPARDY!

NORTH DAKOTA

$200	WHAT IS BISMARCK?	$200
$400	WHAT IS SOUTH DAKOTA?	$400
$600	WHO IS SACAJAWEA?	$600
$800	WHO IS TEDDY ROOSEVELT?	$800
$1000	WHO IS LOUIS L'AMOUR?	$1000

DOUBLE JEOPARDY!

THAI FOOD

THE STAPLE FOOD IN THE NORTH OF THAILAND IS THE STICKY OR GLUTINOUS TYPE OF THIS	**$200**	WHAT IS
TOM KHA KAI IS A CHICKEN SOUP FLAVORED WITH THE "MILK" OF THIS	**$400**	WHAT IS
IN THE NAMES OF NOODLE DISHES, THIS WORD PRECEDES "THAI", "SEE EW" & "WOON SEN"	**$600**	WHAT IS
YOU MIGHT WISH THE SKEWER OF CHICKEN OR BEEF SERVED WITH PEANUT SAUCE WAS "JUST A LITTLE BIT LONGER"	**$800**	WHAT IS
LIKE SOUTHERN COOKING, THAI-AMERICAN CUISINE FEATURES THIS BE"WHISKERED" CREATURE, DEEP-FRIED	**$1000**	WHAT IS

DOUBLE JEOPARDY!

THAI FOOD

$200	WHAT IS RICE?	**$200**
$400	WHAT IS COCONUT?	**$400**
$600	WHAT IS PAD?	**$600**
$800	WHAT IS A SATAY?	**$800**
$1000	WHAT IS CATFISH?	**$1000**

DOUBLE JEOPARDY!

THE THEATRE

LAURENCE HARVEY REIGNED IN THIS REGAL ROLE IN THE 1964 LONDON PRODUCTION OF "CAMELOT"	**$200**	WHO IS
NOEL COWARD'S 1947 DRAMA "PEACE IN OUR TIME" DEPICTS LIFE IN ENGLAND IF THIS DICTATOR HAD CONQUERED IT	**$400**	WHO IS
CHEKHOV'S "THREE SISTERS" DREAM OF GOING TO THIS CAPITAL CITY	**$600**	WHAT IS
SEWAMONO PLAYS ARE DOMESTIC DRAMAS ABOUT MIDDLE-CLASS LIFE IN THIS FORM OF JAPANESE DRAMA	**$800**	WHAT IS
IN 1999 CRITICS LAMBASTED "TALLER THAN A DWARF", WRITTEN BY THIS EX-PARTNER OF MIKE NICHOLS	**$1000**	WHO IS

71

DOUBLE JEOPARDY!

THE THEATRE

$200	WHO IS KING ARTHUR?	$200
$400	WHO IS ADOLF HITLER?	$400
$600	WHAT IS MOSCOW?	$600
$800	WHAT IS KABUKI?	$800
$1000	WHO IS ELAINE MAY?	$1000

DOUBLE JEOPARDY!

THE YEAR OF THE HEADLINE

ORDERS SKYROCKET AS VIAGRA GOES ON THE MARKET!	**$200**	WHAT IS
U.S. ABANDONS SAIGON; VIETNAM WAR ENDS!	**$400**	WHAT IS
OPERATION "DESERT STORM" BEGINS; IRAQ INVADED!	**$600**	WHAT IS
MONDALE NOMINATED FOR U.S. PRESIDENT!	**$800**	WHAT IS
QUEEN VICTORIA SHUFFLES OFF THIS MORTAL COIL!	**$1000**	WHAT IS

DOUBLE JEOPARDY!

THE YEAR OF THE HEADLINE

$200	WHAT IS 1998?	**$200**
$400	WHAT IS 1975?	**$400**
$600	WHAT IS 1991?	**$600**
$800	WHAT IS 1984?	**$800**
$1000	WHAT IS 1901?	**$1000**

DOUBLE JEOPARDY!

VANS

COLUMNIST ABIGAIL, OPPOSED TO SMOKING, OR PRESIDENT MARTIN, OPPOSED TO THE ANNEXATION OF TEXAS	**$200**	WHO IS
GAME SHOW PRODUCERS ONCE QUAKED AT THE NAME OF THIS 1950s COLUMBIA UNIVERSITY INSTRUCTOR	**$400**	WHO IS
THIS "MOONDANCE" SINGER WAS ONCE MARRIED TO A WOMAN NAMED JANET PLANET	**$600**	WHO IS
LAST NAME OF "WATERMELON MAN" DIRECTOR MELVIN & HIS SON, "NEW JACK CITY" DIRECTOR MARIO	**$800**	WHAT IS
SHE SET AN AMERICAN RECORD IN 1996 BY SWIMMING THE 50-METER FREESTYLE IN 24.87 SECONDS	**$1000**	WHO IS

DOUBLE JEOPARDY!

VANS

$200   WHO IS VAN BUREN? $200

$400   WHO IS CHARLES VAN DOREN? $400

$600   WHO IS VAN MORRISON? $600

$800   WHAT IS VAN PEEBLES? $800

$1000   WHO IS AMY VAN DYKEN? $1000

FINAL JEOPARDY!

ITALIAN VOCABULARY

THIS WORD WELL KNOWN
TO SCULPTURE LOVERS
CAN BE TRANSLATED AS
"MERCY" OR "COMPASSION"

WHAT IS

FINAL JEOPARDY!

ITALIAN VOCABULARY

WHAT IS PIETA?

JEOPARDY!

THE PC

BYZANTINE PRIESTS MIGHT KNOW THE NAME OF THESE SCREEN IMAGES THAT CAN REPRESENT PROGRAMS OR FILES	$100	WHAT ARE
ONE OF THESE IS EQUAL TO 1,024 BYTES	$200	WHAT IS
TO TAKE FLEAS OFF YOUR DOG, OR TO DETECT, LOCATE & CORRECT ERRORS IN A COMPUTER PROGRAM	$300	WHAT IS
"SMALL" TERM FOR A CENTRAL PROCESSING UNIT ON ONE INTEGRATED CIRCUIT	$400	WHAT IS
IT'S NOT A SPIDER, IT'S THE PERSON RESPONSIBLE FOR MAINTAINING AN INTERNET SITE	$500	WHAT IS

JEOPARDY!

THE PC

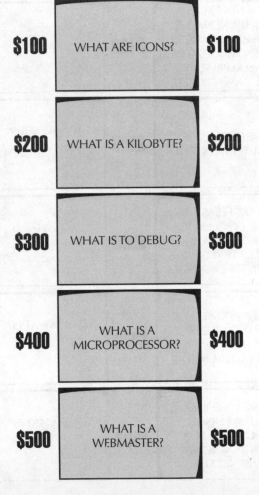

$100   WHAT ARE ICONS? $100

$200   WHAT IS A KILOBYTE? $200

$300   WHAT IS TO DEBUG? $300

$400   WHAT IS A MICROPROCESSOR? $400

$500   WHAT IS A WEBMASTER? $500

JEOPARDY!

AROUND THE PACIFIC

2 OF CHILE'S JUAN FERNANDEZ ISLANDS ARE NAMED FOR ALEXANDER SELKIRK & THIS FICTIONAL CASTAWAY HE INSPIRED	**$100**	WHO IS
THIS RIVER IN WASHINGTON & OREGON WAS EXPLORED BY ROBERT GRAY IN A SHIP OF THE SAME NAME	**$200**	WHAT IS
IN 1697 JESUITS FOUNDED LORETO, THE 1st PERMANENT EUROPEAN SETTLEMENT ON THIS "LOWER" PENINSULA	**$300**	WHAT IS
THE ISLAND OF MINDANAO IS A MUSLIM CENTER IN THIS MAINLY ROMAN CATHOLIC COUNTRY	**$400**	WHAT IS
TO CALL THE ROTORUA MAN, YOU'LL HAVE TO RING UP THIS ANTIPODEAN ISLAND NATION	**$500**	WHAT IS

JEOPARDY!™

AROUND THE PACIFIC

$100	WHO IS ROBINSON CRUSOE?	$100
$200	WHAT IS THE COLUMBIA?	$200
$300	WHAT IS LOWER (OR BAJA) CALIFORNIA?	$300
$400	WHAT IS THE PHILIPPINES?	$400
$500	WHAT IS NEW ZEALAND?	$500

JEOPARDY!

COCKNEY RHYMING SLANG

Clue	Value	Response
IT'S A DICKORY DOCK, WHETHER OR NOT A MOUSE RUNS UP IT	**$100**	WHAT IS
ASK A COCKNEY BARBER FOR A DIG IN THE GRAVE & HE SHOULD GIVE YOU ONE OF THESE	**$200**	WHAT IS
IT'S WHAT A MOTHER HUBBARD IS; HERS WAS BARE, BY THE WAY	**$300**	WHAT IS
A GLASGOW RANGER, THIS KIND OF PERSON, WASN'T WELCOME IN SMALL TOWNS IN THE OLD WEST	**$400**	WHAT IS
COCKNEYS USE THE NAME OF THIS DICKENS TITLE CHARACTER AS RHYMING SLANG FOR A JUDGE	**$500**	WHO IS

JEOPARDY!

COCKNEY RHYMING SLANG

$100	WHAT IS A CLOCK?	$100
$200	WHAT IS A SHAVE?	$200
$300	WHAT IS A CUPBOARD?	$300
$400	WHAT IS A STRANGER?	$400
$500	WHO IS BARNABY RUDGE?	$500

JEOPARDY!

GEOGRAPHIC TERMS

THIS LINE DIVIDES THE EARTH INTO NORTHERN & SOUTHERN HEMISPHERES	**$100**	WHAT IS
TILL IS DEFINED AS THE ROCK MATERIAL DRAGGED UNDER ONE OF THESE AS IT MOVES	**$200**	WHAT IS
A BODY OF WATER USUALLY SMALLER THAN A GULF; BOTANY IS A FAMOUS ONE	**$300**	WHAT IS
NORMALLY, AN ATOLL IS MADE OF THIS OR NOTHING ATOLL	**$400**	WHAT IS
A COMMON PLACE NAME IN THE SOUTHWEST, FROM A SPANISH TERM, IT'S A DRY RIVER BED	**$500**	WHAT IS

JEOPARDY!

GEOGRAPHIC TERMS

$100 — WHAT IS THE EQUATOR? — $100

$200 — WHAT IS A GLACIER? — $200

$300 — WHAT IS A BAY? — $300

$400 — WHAT IS CORAL? — $400

$500 — WHAT IS AN ARROYO? — $500

JEOPARDY!™

SIMONIZING

BORN IN 1927, HE WROTE HIS FIRST BROADWAY HIT, "COME BLOW YOUR HORN", IN 1960	**$100**	WHO IS
FROM 1972 TO 1983, SHE WAS MRS. JAMES TAYLOR	**$200**	WHO IS
HARRIET BEECHER STOWE'S SINISTER SLAVER	**$300**	WHO IS
HE WON THE DEMOCRATIC PRESIDENTIAL PRIMARY IN ILLINOIS IN 1988; NO BIG SURPRISE, HE WAS THEIR SENATOR	**$400**	WHO IS
HE'S THE LEAD SINGER & OLDEST MEMBER OF DURAN DURAN	**$500**	WHO IS

JEOPARDY!

SIMONIZING

$100	WHO IS NEIL SIMON?	**$100**
$200	WHO IS CARLY SIMON?	**$200**
$300	WHO IS SIMON LEGREE?	**$300**
$400	WHO IS PAUL SIMON?	**$400**
$500	WHO IS SIMON LE BON?	**$500**

JEOPARDY!

PRESIDENTIAL LAST WORDS

JUST BEFORE COLLAPSING IN 1945, HE REMARKED, "I HAVE A TERRIFIC HEADACHE"	**$100**	WHO IS
"IT IS WELL" WERE HIS LAST WORDS IN 1799	**$200**	WHO IS
IN 1885, HE CROAKED, "WATER!"	**$300**	WHO IS
IN 1969 HE ENDED HIS TOUR OF DUTY WITH "I HAVE ALWAYS LOVED MY COUNTRY"	**$400**	WHO IS
IN 1893 HAYES GASPED, "I KNOW THAT I AM GOING TO WHERE" THIS WIFE "IS"	**$500**	WHO IS

JEOPARDY!™

PRESIDENTIAL LAST WORDS

$100 — WHO IS FRANKLIN DELANO ROOSEVELT? — $100

$200 — WHO IS GEORGE WASHINGTON? — $200

$300 — WHO IS ULYSSES S. GRANT? — $300

$400 — WHO IS DWIGHT D. EISENHOWER? — $400

$500 — WHO IS LUCY? — $500

DOUBLE JEOPARDY!

NAMES IN THE LAW

THE CIVIL CODE SET UP IN FRANCE IN 1804 IS ALSO KNOWN AS THIS CODE	**$200**	WHAT IS
EARL WARREN RULED ON THIS MAN'S CASE THAT A SUSPECT MUST BE WARNED PRIOR TO QUESTIONING THAT HE CAN STAY SILENT	**$400**	WHO IS
IN 1970 A WOMAN USED THIS PSEUDO-NYM WHEN SHE SUED TEXAS D.A. HENRY WADE TO ALLOW HER AN ABORTION	**$600**	WHAT IS
HE TOOK ON FERGUSON IN 1896 AFTER REFUSING TO SIT IN THE RAILROAD CAR FOR BLACKS ONLY	**$800**	WHO IS
THE 1936 ROBINSON-PATMAN ACT REVIVED & REVISED THIS MAN'S ANTITRUST ACT OF 1890	**$1000**	WHO IS

DOUBLE JEOPARDY!

NAMES IN THE LAW

$200	WHAT IS THE NAPOLEONIC CODE? **$200**
$400	WHO IS ERNESTO MIRANDA? **$400**
$600	WHAT IS JANE ROE? **$600**
$800	WHO IS HOMER PLESSY? **$800**
$1000	WHO IS JOHN SHERMAN? **$1000**

DOUBLE JEOPARDY!

CLASSIC DRAMA

IT INCLUDES THE FORESHADOWING LINE "HEDDA DARLING— DON'T TOUCH THOSE DANGEROUS THINGS!"	**$200**	WHAT IS
HE'S THE KING OR "REX" WHO SAVES THEBES IN AN ANCIENT WORK BY SOPHOCLES	**$400**	WHO IS
PIERRE CORNEILLE WROTE A 1637 PLAY ABOUT THIS MEDIEVAL SPANISH HERO	**$600**	WHO IS
SHAKESPEAREAN WOMAN WHO ASKS, "WHERE IS THE BEAU-TEOUS MAJESTY OF DENMARK?"	**$800**	WHO IS
THE WORKS OF THIS 17th C. FRENCHMAN, INCLUDING "ANDRO-MACHE" & "PHAEDRA", ARE KNOWN FOR THEIR LACK OF ACTION	**$1000**	WHO IS

DOUBLE JEOPARDY!

CLASSIC DRAMA

$200	WHAT IS "HEDDA GABLER"?	**$200**
$400	WHO IS OEDIPUS?	**$400**
$600	WHO IS EL CID?	**$600**
$800	WHO IS OPHELIA?	**$800**
$1000	WHO IS JEAN RACINE?	**$1000**

DOUBLE JEOPARDY!

GOOD SPORTS

Clue	Value	Response
THIS BIG FELLA AVERAGED 55 HOME RUNS IN 1996 & 1997, BUT WAS JUST GETTING WARMED UP	$200	WHO IS
HE CONQUERED CANCER TO BECOME ONLY THE SECOND AMERICAN TO WIN THE TOUR DE FRANCE	$400	WHO IS
HIS 1990 KNOCKOUT OF MIKE TYSON HAS BEEN CALLED THE GREATEST HEAVY-WEIGHT TITLE UPSET	$600	WHO IS
THIS "GODDESS" BEAT LINDSAY DAVENPORT AT WIMBLEDON 2000 FOR HER FIRST GRAND SLAM SINGLES TITLE	$800	WHO IS
THIS VETERAN BOSTON DEFENSEMAN WENT TO COLORADO IN 2000 TO TRY TO WIN A STANLEY CUP	$1000	WHO IS

DOUBLE JEOPARDY!

GOOD SPORTS

$200	WHO IS MARK McGWIRE?	**$200**
$400	WHO IS LANCE ARMSTRONG?	**$400**
$600	WHO IS JAMES "BUSTER" DOUGLAS?	**$600**
$800	WHO IS VENUS WILLIAMS?	**$800**
$1000	WHO IS RAYMOND BOURQUE?	**$1000**

DOUBLE JEOPARDY!

WORLD HODGEPODGE

IN ITALY, A KINDLY WITCH CALLED BEFANA DELIVERS CHRISTMAS GIFTS, RIDING FROM HOUSE TO HOUSE ON ONE OF THESE	$200	WHAT IS
THE BHARATA NATYAM IS A HIGHLY STYLIZED DANCE THAT ORIGINATED IN THIS COUNTRY	$400	WHAT IS
AZERI IS THE OFFICIAL LANGUAGE OF THIS COUNTRY	$600	WHAT IS
ASSINIBOINE PARK IN THIS CAPITAL OF MANITOBA BOASTS A MINIATURE RAILWAY	$800	WHAT IS
MISS UNIVERSE 1992, MICHELLE McLEAN, FOUNDED A CHILDREN'S TRUST IN THIS COUNTRY ONCE KNOWN AS SOUTH WEST AFRICA	$1000	WHAT IS

DOUBLE JEOPARDY!

WORLD HODGEPODGE

$200	WHAT IS A BROOMSTICK?	**$200**
$400	WHAT IS INDIA?	**$400**
$600	WHAT IS AZERBAIJAN?	**$600**
$800	WHAT IS WINNEPEG?	**$800**
$1000	WHAT IS NAMIBIA?	**$1000**

DOUBLE JEOPARDY!

U.S. U.N. REPS

5 YEARS AFTER EISEN-HOWER DEFEATED HIM A SECOND TIME, HE PACKED HIS BAGS & HEADED TO THE U.N.	**$200**	WHO IS
HE WENT FROM THE U.N. IN 1976 TO THE U.S. SENATE REPRE-SENTING NEW YORK IN 1977	**$400**	WHO IS
THIS MAN FROM NEW MEXICO WENT FROM THE U.N. TO THE POST OF SECRETARY OF ENERGY UNDER CLINTON	**$600**	WHO IS
IN 1981 SHE BECAME THE FIRST WOMAN THE U.S. PUT INTO THE POST	**$800**	WHO IS
IN 1960 HE WAS A U.N. AMBASSADOR & NIXON'S RUNNING MATE	**$1000**	WHO IS

DOUBLE JEOPARDY!

U.S. U.N. REPS

$200 — WHO IS ADLAI STEVENSON? — $200

$400 — WHO IS DANIEL PATRICK MOYNIHAN? — $400

$600 — WHO IS BILL RICHARDSON? — $600

$800 — WHO IS JEANE J. KIRKPATRICK? — $800

$1000 — WHO IS HENRY CABOT LODGE, JR.? — $1000

DOUBLE JEOPARDY!

ENDS IN "LE"

TO LOSE CONTROL OF THE PIGSKIN	**$200**	WHAT IS
PROVERBIALLY, TO DALLY IN THE FACE OF A CRISIS IS TO DO THIS "WHILE ROME BURNS"	**$400**	WHAT IS
IF YOU'RE GONNA SET ON THE PORCH FOR A SPELL, YOU'LL WANT TO DO THIS TO SHAPE PIECES OF WOOD	**$600**	WHAT IS
SOME BIRDS ARE NAMED FOR THE ABILITY TO DO THIS, SING WITH TRILLS & QUAVERS	**$800**	WHAT IS
FROM OLD ENGLISH FOR "DART", IT MEANS TO MOVE BACK & FORTH BETWEEN 2 PLACES—PERHAPS EARTH & SPACE	**$1000**	WHAT IS

DOUBLE JEOPARDY!

ENDS IN "LE"

$200	WHAT IS FUMBLE?	**$200**
$400	WHAT IS FIDDLE?	**$400**
$600	WHAT IS WHITTLE?	**$600**
$800	WHAT IS WARBLE?	**$800**
$1000	WHAT IS SHUTTLE?	**$1000**

FINAL JEOPARDY!

FAMOUS FATHERS

HE PLAYED RHYTHM &
BLUES GUITAR BEFORE
WORKING AS A CRANE
OPERATOR & RAISING A
FAMILY IN GARY, INDIANA

WHO IS

FINAL JEOPARDY!

FAMOUS FATHERS

WHO IS JOSEPH JACKSON?

JEOPARDY!

THE BAD OLD DAYS

IT WASN'T A COLLEGE FOOTBALL GAME, IT WAS THE GREAT PLAINS AREA RACKED BY DROUGHT IN THE 1930s	**$100**	WHAT IS
1950s COLLEGE BASKETBALL WAS HIT BY SCANDAL WHEN PLAYERS WERE "RAZOR"-SHARP AT THIS ACTIVITY	**$200**	WHAT IS
THE SCANDALS OF HIS 1920s PRESIDENCY INCLUDED SKIMMING BY VETERANS BUREAU HEAD CHARLES FORBES	**$300**	WHO IS
THE FOUNDING OF THIS ORGANIZATION IN 1909 WAS SPURRED BY A SPRINGFIELD, ILL. RACE RIOT THE PREVIOUS YEAR	**$400**	WHAT IS
ORIGINALLY MEANING "FOREIGNERS", IT REFERS TO THOSE WHO OVERRAN THE ROMAN EMPIRE & BEGAN THE DARK AGES	**$500**	WHO ARE

JEOPARDY!

THE BAD OLD DAYS

$100	WHAT IS THE DUST BOWL?	$100
$200	WHAT IS POINT SHAVING?	$200
$300	WHO IS WARREN G. HARDING?	$300
$400	WHAT IS THE NAACP?	$400
$500	WHO ARE BARBARIANS?	$500

JEOPARDY!

ENDS IN "ELLA"

CHEESE FOR PIZZA	$100	WHAT IS
CHARLES PERRAULT'S VERSION ADDED THE GLASS SLIPPER TO HER STORY	$200	WHO IS
NAME SHOUTED IN THE CONCLUSION OF THE FILM "A STREETCAR NAMED DESIRE"	$300	WHAT IS
BACTERIA OFTEN FOUND IN CONTAM-INATED FOOD, NOT JUST CERTAIN FISH	$400	WHAT IS
ACTRESS SCIORRA	$500	WHO IS

JEOPARDY!

ENDS IN "ELLA"

$100	WHAT IS MOZZARELLA?	$100
$200	WHO IS CINDERELLA?	$200
$300	WHAT IS "STELLA"?	$300
$400	WHAT IS SALMONELLA?	$400
$500	WHO IS ANNABELLA?	$500

JEOPARDY!

STATE CAPITALS

MUSICALLY, THIS CAPITAL IS KNOWN FOR ITS "POPS" CONCERTS & SUMMER CONCERTS ON THE CHARLES RIVER ESPLANADE	**$100**	WHAT IS
THIS SMALL CAPITAL LIES AT THE WESTERN EDGE OF ITS STATE'S BLUEGRASS REGION	**$200**	WHAT IS
IT WAS THE ORIGINAL WESTERN TERMINUS OF THE TRANSCONTINENTAL RAILROAD	**$300**	WHAT IS
A STATUE OF ETHAN ALLEN GRACES THE CAPITOL BUILDING PORTICO IN THIS CITY	**$400**	WHAT IS
THIS CAPITAL'S EXECUTIVE MANSION WAS ONCE THE HOME OF JAMES G. BLAINE	**$500**	WHAT IS

JEOPARDY!

STATE CAPITALS

$100	WHAT IS BOSTON?	$100
$200	WHAT IS FRANKFORT?	$200
$300	WHAT IS SACRAMENTO?	$300
$400	WHAT IS MONTPELIER?	$400
$500	WHAT IS AUGUSTA?	$500

JEOPARDY!

FOOD STUFF

IT'S NO FISH STORY: CIOPPINO IS A FISH STEW FROM THIS CITY'S FISHERMAN'S WHARF	**$100**	WHAT IS
THIS CUT OF BEEF THAT'S ALSO A MAN'S NICKNAME COMES FROM BETWEEN THE NECK & THE SHOULDER BLADE	**$200**	WHAT IS
BEURRE BERCY IS MADE WITH WHITE WINE, SHALLOTS, DICED BEEF MARROW, PARSLEY, & OF COURSE, THIS SPREAD	**$300**	WHAT IS
THIS TART, YELLOWISH LIME THAT'S NATIVE TO FLORIDA IS THE MAIN INGREDIENT IN A POPULAR PIE	**$400**	WHAT IS
IN SCOTLAND THESE "COLORFUL" BERRIES ARE CALLED BRAM-BLES, & SCOTS MAKE BRAMBLE WINE FROM THEM	**$500**	WHAT ARE

JEOPARDY!

FOOD STUFF

$100	WHAT IS SAN FRANCISCO?	$100
$200	WHAT IS CHUCK?	$200
$300	WHAT IS BUTTER?	$300
$400	WHAT IS KEY LIME?	$400
$500	WHAT ARE BLACKBERRIES?	$500

JEOPARDY!

SPORTS MEDICINE

THE "STRESS" TYPE IS A HAIRLINE BREAK CAUSED BY OVERUSE	**$100**	WHAT IS
IN TENDINITIS & BURSITIS, -ITIS DENOTES THIS	**$200**	WHAT IS
A TEAR TO THE ACL, OR ANTERIOR CRUCIATE ONE OF THESE IN THE KNEE, HAS BROUGHT MANY ATHLETES TO THEIR KNEES	**$300**	WHAT IS
THEY'RE THE MUSCLES THAT FLEX THE KNEE: PIGS PROBABLY DON'T INJURE THEIRS AS OFTEN AS HUMANS DO	**$400**	WHAT ARE
TO PRO ATHLETES, A "SCOPE" IS USUALLY SHORT FOR THIS TYPE OF DEVICE TO VIEW THE INTERIOR OF A JOINT CAVITY	**$500**	WHAT IS

JEOPARDY!

SPORTS MEDICINE

$100	WHAT IS A FRACTURE?	$100
$200	WHAT IS INFLAMMATION?	$200
$300	WHAT IS LIGAMENT?	$300
$400	WHAT ARE HAMSTRINGS?	$400
$500	WHAT IS ARTHROSCOPE?	$500

JEOPARDY!

NEWSMEN/AUTHORS

IN 1997's "A REPORTER'S LIFE" HE COVERED HIS 31 YEARS AT CBS NEWS	$100	WHO IS
THIS NBC ANCHOR'S "THE GREATEST GENERATION" PAID TRIBUTE TO THOSE WHO CAME OF AGE DURING WORLD WAR II	$200	WHO IS
IN 1998 THIS ABC ANCHOR, ALONG WITH TODD BREWSTER, TOOK ON "THE CENTURY"	$300	WHO IS
HE & KYLE GIBSON WROTE "NIGHTLINE: HISTORY IN THE MAKING AND THE MAKING OF TELEVISION"	$400	WHO IS
"EVERYONE IS ENTITLED TO MY OPINION" COLLECTED HIS COMMENTARIES FROM "THIS WEEK"	$500	WHO IS

JEOPARDY!

NEWSMEN/AUTHORS

$100	WHO IS WALTER CRONKITE?	$100
$200	WHO IS TOM BROKAW?	$200
$300	WHO IS PETER JENNINGS?	$300
$400	WHO IS TED KOPPEL?	$400
$500	WHO IS DAVID BRINKLEY?	$500

DOUBLE JEOPARDY!

LITERARY OPENINGS

THIS SEUSS TALE BEGINS, "EVERY WHO DOWN IN WHO-VILLE LIKED CHRISTMAS A LOT . . ."	**$200**	WHAT IS
THE STORY OF THIS UNHAPPY RUSSIAN WOMAN BEGINS WITH A FAMOUS REMARK ABOUT HAPPY & UNHAPPY FAMILIES	**$400**	WHO IS
HIS "THE MALTESE FALCON" OPENS "SAMUEL SPADE'S JAW WAS LONG AND BONY"	**$600**	WHO IS
"IT WAS A PLEASURE TO BURN" BEGINS THIS RAY BRADBURY BOOK WITH A TEMPER-ATURE FOR ITS TITLE	**$800**	WHAT IS
THIS FRENCH AUTHOR'S "THE STRANGER" LACONICALLY BEGINS, "MY MOTHER DIED. TODAY, OR MAYBE IT WAS YESTERDAY."	**$1000**	WHO IS

DOUBLE JEOPARDY!

LITERARY OPENINGS

$200	WHAT IS "HOW THE GRINCH STOLE CHRISTMAS"?	**$200**
$400	WHO IS ANNA KARENINA?	**$400**
$600	WHO IS DASHIELL HAMMETT?	**$600**
$800	WHAT IS "FAHRENHEIT 451"?	**$800**
$1000	WHO IS ALBERT CAMUS?	**$1000**

DOUBLE JEOPARDY!™

COLLEGE TEAM NICKNAMES

DIFFERENT CAMPUSES OF THE UNIVERSITY OF THIS STATE ARE HOME TO ANTEATERS, BANANA SLUGS & GOLDEN BEARS	**$200**	WHAT IS
THIS WORD PRECEDES THE IRISH OF NOTRE DAME & THE ILLINI OF THE UNIVERSITY OF ILLINOIS	**$400**	WHAT IS
THIS CANINE REPRESENTS OVER 30 COLLEGES IN-CLUDING YALE & THE UNIVERSITY OF GEORGIA	**$600**	WHAT IS
THE MEN'S TEAMS AT NORTHLAND COLLEGE IN WISCON-SIN ARE THE LUMBER-JACKS & THE WOMEN'S TEAMS ARE THESE	**$800**	WHO ARE
OHIO STATE HONORS EACH OF ITS ALL-AMERICANS BY PLANT-ING ONE OF THESE MASCOT TREES IN A GROVE	**$1000**	WHAT ARE

DOUBLE JEOPARDY!
COLLEGE TEAM NICKNAMES

$200	WHAT IS CALIFORNIA?	**$200**
$400	WHAT IS FIGHTING?	**$400**
$600	WHAT IS THE BULLDOG?	**$600**
$800	WHO ARE THE LUMBERJILLS?	**$800**
$1000	WHAT ARE BUCKEYES?	**$1000**

DOUBLE JEOPARDY!

IT'S JAPANESE TO ME

JAPAN'S CURRENCY IS CALLED THIS, MEANING "ROUND", AS OPPOSED TO EARLIER COINS, WHICH WERE OFTEN SQUARE	**$200**	WHAT IS
"ARIGATO" IS JAPANESE FOR THIS & "DOMO ARIGATO GOZAI-MASHTA" IS JAPANESE FOR THIS "VERY MUCH"	**$400**	WHAT IS
THE GREEN TYPE OF THIS BEVERAGE IS CALLED AGARI, "FINISHED"	**$600**	WHAT IS
THESE FEMALE ENTERTAINERS ARE FOUND IN THE KARYUKAI, "FLOWER & WILLOW WORLD"	**$800**	WHAT ARE
WHEN YOU TRY TO CATCH THESE CULTIVATED CARP, YOU'D EXPECT THEM TO PLAY HARD TO GET	**$1000**	WHAT ARE

DOUBLE JEOPARDY!

IT'S JAPANESE TO ME

$200	WHAT IS THE YEN?	$200
$400	WHAT IS THANK YOU?	$400
$600	WHAT IS TEA?	$600
$800	WHAT ARE GEISHA?	$800
$1000	WHAT ARE KOI?	$1000

DOUBLE JEOPARDY!

TV MINISERIES

YOU COULD CALL HENRY THOMAS ISHMAEL & PATRICK STEWART AHAB IN THIS 1998 MINISERIES	**$200**	WHAT IS
VANESSA WILLIAMS PLAYED CALYPSO & GRETA SCACCHI WAS THE LONG-SUFFERING PENELOPE IN THIS 1997 EPIC	**$400**	WHAT IS
THE 2000 MINISERIES ABOUT THIS "KING-DOM" FEATURED CAMRYN MANHEIM AS SNOW WHITE	**$600**	WHAT IS
ROBERT DUVALL SAT TALL IN THE SADDLE AS AUGUSTUS McCRAE IN THIS 1989 4-PART WESTERN	**$800**	WHAT IS
IN 1994 STEPHEN COLLINS PLAYED ASHLEY WILKES IN THIS MINISERIES SEQUEL TO "GONE WITH THE WIND"	**$1000**	WHAT IS

DOUBLE JEOPARDY!

TV MINISERIES

$200	WHAT IS "MOBY DICK"?	**$200**
$400	WHAT IS "THE ODYSSEY"?	**$400**
$600	WHAT IS "THE 10th KINGDOM"?	**$600**
$800	WHAT IS "LONESOME DOVE"?	**$800**
$1000	WHAT IS "SCARLETT"?	**$1000**

DOUBLE JEOPARDY!

PHARAOHS

LORD CARNARVON REPORTEDLY CALLED THIS RULER'S TOMB "THE GREATEST SIGHT I HAVE EVER WITNESSED"	**$200**	WHO IS
WHILE ONLY A PRINCE, TUTHMOSIS IV HAD THIS COLOSSAL STATUE OF GIZA RESTORED	**$400**	WHAT IS
THIS ANCIENT CAPITAL GREW UP AROUND PEPI I's PYRAMID, MEN-NEFER-MARE	**$600**	WHAT IS
2-WORD NAME FOR THE SITE SOUTH OF CAIRO WHERE RAMSES II BUILT 2 SANDSTONE TEMPLES	**$800**	WHAT IS
NAME SHARED BY THE SECOND KING OF THE 19th DYNASTY & THE SEARCH FOR EXTRATERRESTRIAL INTELLIGENCE	**$1000**	WHAT IS

DOUBLE JEOPARDY!

PHARAOHS

$200	WHO IS KING TUT?	$200
$400	WHAT IS THE (GREAT) SPHINX?	$400
$600	WHAT IS MEMPHIS?	$600
$800	WHAT IS ABU SIMBEL?	$800
$1000	WHAT IS SETI?	$1000

DOUBLE JEOPARDY!

NEW YORK BUILDINGS

ITS ARCHITECT, WILLIAM VAN ALEN, WAS "DRIVEN" TO CREATE THE WORLD'S TALLEST BUILDING AT THAT TIME	**$200**	WHAT IS
THIS BUILDING, JOHN LENNON'S LAST RESIDENCE, WAS SO NAMED BECAUSE 72nd ST. SEEMED LIKE THE FAR WEST	**$400**	WHAT IS
THE OLD RCA BUILDING AT 30 ROCKEFELLER PLAZA IS NOW CALLED THIS "BUILDING", ONE INITIAL SHORTER	**$600**	WHAT IS
THE BUILDING NAMED FOR THIS RETAILER INCLUDES A SCULPTURE OF HIM COUNTING NICKELS & DIMES	**$800**	WHO IS
NAMED FOR ITS DEVELOPER, THIS MIDTOWN TOWER HAS AN ATRIUM WITH A WATERFALL INSTEAD OF A MERE LOBBY	**$1000**	WHAT IS

DOUBLE JEOPARDY!

NEW YORK BUILDINGS

$200	WHAT IS THE CHRYSLER BUILDING?	**$200**
$400	WHAT IS THE DAKOTA?	**$400**
$600	WHAT IS THE GE BUILDING?	**$600**
$800	WHO IS F. W. WOOLWORTH?	**$800**
$1000	WHAT IS TRUMP TOWER?	**$1000**

SONGWRITERS

IT WAS ONCE SAID OF THIS MAN WHO LIVED TO BE 101: HE "HAS NO PLACE IN AMERICAN MUSIC. HE IS AMERICAN MUSIC"

WHO IS

FINAL JEOPARDY!

SONGWRITERS

WHO IS IRVING BERLIN?

JEOPARDY!

FAMOUS WOMEN

NICKNAME OF AL GORE'S WIFE MARY ELIZABETH	$100	WHAT IS
CINDY CRAWFORD IS ONE OF "THE MOST UNFORGETTABLE WOMEN IN THE WORLD" WI IO WEAR THIS MAKEUP BRAND	$200	WHAT IS
IN 1998 TARA LIPINSKI REPLACED THIS NORWEGIAN LASS AS THE YOUNGEST OLYMPIC FIGURE SKATING CHAMP	$300	WHO IS
ONCE A MEMBER OF THE "BRAT PACK", SHE RETURNED TO THE BIG SCREEN AS A PHOTOGRAPHER IN 1998's "HIGH ART"	$400	WHO IS
THIS UNFORTUNATELY NAMED WOMAN WHO FOUNDED THE HOUSTON SYMPHONY NEVER HAD A SISTER NAMED URA HOGG	$500	WHO IS

JEOPARDY!

FAMOUS WOMEN

$100	WHAT IS TIPPER?	**$100**
$200	WHAT IS REVLON?	**$200**
$300	WHO IS SONJA HENIE?	**$300**
$400	WHO IS ALLY SHEEDY?	**$400**
$500	WHO IS IMA HOGG?	**$500**

JEOPARDY!

THE NORMANS

Clue	Value	Response
THE NORMANS CALLED THEIR KNIGHTS THIS; ONE MAY HAVE BEEN MAURICE'S ANCESTOR	$100	WHAT ARE
IT TAKES A FIEF TO RUN THIS SYSTEM THAT THE NORMANS LEARNED FROM THE CAROLINGIANS	$200	WHAT IS
THIS BATTLE OF OCTOBER 14, 1066 ESTABLISHED THE NORMANS AS RULERS OF ENGLAND	$300	WHAT IS
NORMAN CRUSADER TANCRED OF HAUTE-VILLE BECAME PRINCE OF THIS REGION OF PALESTINE KNOWN FOR ITS SEA	$400	WHAT IS
THE FIRST NORMAN FOOTHOLD IN FRANCE WAS NEAR THIS CITY WHERE JOAN OF ARC MET HER END	$500	WHAT IS

133

JEOPARDY!

THE NORMANS

$100	WHAT ARE CHEVALIERS?
$200	WHAT IS THE FEUDAL SYSTEM?
$300	WHAT IS THE BATTLE OF HASTINGS?
$400	WHAT IS GALILEE?
$500	WHAT IS ROUEN?

JEOPARDY!

NATIONAL AIRLINES

ACCORDING TO "RAIN MAN", THIS AUSSIE AIRLINE IS THE ONLY ONE THAT NEVER CRASHED	$100	WHAT IS
YOU'LL FEEL LIKE A GOD ON OLYMPIC AIRWAYS, THIS COUNTRY'S NATIONAL AIRLINE	$200	WHAT IS
ALL FOOD IS STRICTLY KOSHER ON THIS NATIONAL AIRLINE ESTABLISHED IN 1949	$300	WHAT IS
LUXAIR AIRLINES IS THE NATIONAL CARRIER OF THIS GRAND DUCHY	$400	WHAT IS
ENGLISH INITIALS OF THE NATIONAL AIRLINE OF THE NETHERLANDS	$500	WHAT IS

JEOPARDY!

NATIONAL AIRLINES

$100 WHAT IS QANTAS? $100

$200 WHAT IS GREECE? $200

$300 WHAT IS EL AL? $300

$400 WHAT IS LUXEMBOURG? $400

$500 WHAT IS KLM? $500

JEOPARDY!

CROSSWORD CLUES "T"

DOROTHY'S DOGGIE (4)	**$100**	WHO IS
SURF'S PARTNER, ON A MENU (4)	**$200**	WHAT IS
BOW, OR BOLO (3)	**$300**	WHAT IS
SALTWATER SWEET (5)	**$400**	WHAT IS
HITCHHIKING ESSENTIAL (5)	**$500**	WHAT IS

JEOPARDY!

CROSSWORD CLUES "T"

$100	WHO IS TOTO?	$100
$200	WHAT IS TURF?	$200
$300	WHAT IS A TIE?	$300
$400	WHAT IS TAFFY?	$400
$500	WHAT IS A THUMB?	$500

JEOPARDY!

U.S. BODIES OF WATER

THE CHICAGO RIVER ORIGINALLY FLOWED INTO THIS GREAT LAKE; NOW IT FLOWS OUT OF IT	**$100**	WHAT IS
BRINE FLIES & BRINE SHRIMP ARE THE ONLY CREATURES THAT THRIVE IN THIS BODY OF WATER NEAR UTAH'S CAPITAL	**$200**	WHAT IS
YOU'LL FIND THE BIG BRANCH NATIONAL WILDLIFE REFUGE ON THE SHORE OF THIS BIG LAKE IN LOUISIANA	**$300**	WHAT IS
THERE'S A COEUR D'ALENE LAKE & A COEUR D'ALENE RIVER IN THIS STATE	**$400**	WHAT IS
WE HOPE YOU KNOW THAT MOUNT HOPE BAY IN RHODE ISLAND IS AN ARM OF THIS LARGER BAY	**$500**	WHAT IS

JEOPARDY!

U.S. BODIES OF WATER

$100	WHAT IS LAKE MICHIGAN?	**$100**
$200	WHAT IS THE GREAT SALT LAKE?	**$200**
$300	WHAT IS LAKE PONTCHARTRAIN?	**$300**
$400	WHAT IS IDAHO?	**$400**
$500	WHAT IS NARRAGANSETT BAY?	**$500**

JEOPARDY!™

TRUSTY SIDEKICKS

COMIC BOOK SIDEKICK KNOWN AS THE "BOY WONDER"	$100	WHO IS
HE NAVIGATED THE JUNGLE WITH THE AID OF CHEETAH, A CHIMP	$200	WHO IS
HE'S PENN'S SILENT SIDEKICK	$300	WHO IS
PROFESSION OF SHERLOCK HOLMES' FAITHFUL WATSON	$400	WHAT IS
IN 2000 THIS TRUSTY LATE-NIGHT SIDEKICK LEFT CONAN O'BRIEN'S SIDE	$500	WHO IS

JEOPARDY!

TRUSTY SIDEKICKS

$100   WHO IS ROBIN? $100

$200   WHO IS TARZAN? $200

$300   WHO IS TELLER? $300

$400   WHAT IS DOCTOR? $400

$500   WHO IS
ANDY RICHTER? $500

142

DOUBLE JEOPARDY!

FRUIT

THE BING & OTHER SWEET VARIETIES OF THIS FRUIT ARE SELF-STERILE; THEY CANNOT POLLINATE THEMSELVES	$200	WHAT IS
THE BARTLETT TYPE OF THIS FRUIT BEGINS TO RIPEN IN SUMMER; OTHER VARIETIES RIPEN LATER IN THE YEAR	$400	WHAT IS
THIS FRUIT OFTEN ORIGINATES FROM PEACH SEEDS & PEACHES SOMETIMES COME FROM ITS SEEDS	$600	WHAT IS
A CLUSTER, OR HAND, OF THIS FRUIT CONSISTS OF 10–20 FINGERS	$800	WHAT IS
THIS HYBRID OF A TANGERINE & A GRAPEFRUIT COMES IN 2 MAIN VARIETIES: ORLANDO & MINNEOLA	$1000	WHAT IS

143

DOUBLE JEOPARDY!

FRUIT

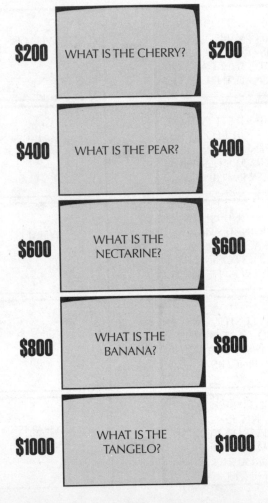

$200 — WHAT IS THE CHERRY? — $200

$400 — WHAT IS THE PEAR? — $400

$600 — WHAT IS THE NECTARINE? — $600

$800 — WHAT IS THE BANANA? — $800

$1000 — WHAT IS THE TANGELO? — $1000

DOUBLE JEOPARDY!

THE ARTICLES OF CONFEDERATION

Clue	Value	Response
THE ARTICLES WERE IN EFFECT FROM 1781 UNTIL REPLACED BY THIS 1787 DOCUMENT	$200	WHAT IS
RICHARD HENRY LEE PROPOSED DRAFTING THE ARTICLES ON JUNE 7 OF THIS YEAR	$400	WHAT IS
UNDER ARTICLE XI THIS PRESENT-DAY COUNTRY COULD HAVE JOINED THE CONFEDERATION JUST BY SIGNING	$600	WHAT IS
THE ARTICLES' LACK OF NATIONAL TAXATION IS CRITICIZED IN NO. 21 OF THESE ESSAYS	$800	WHAT IS
THE "REBELLION" HE LED IN 1786 SHOWED MANY THAT THE ARTICLES DIDN'T INCLUDE A STRONG ENOUGH CENTRAL GOVERNMENT	$1000	WHO IS

DOUBLE JEOPARDY!

THE ARTICLES OF CONFEDERATION

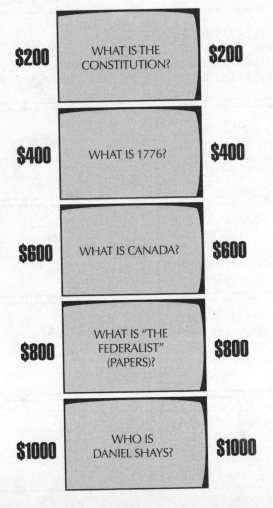

$200   WHAT IS THE CONSTITUTION? $200

$400   WHAT IS 1776? $400

$600   WHAT IS CANADA? $600

$800   WHAT IS "THE FEDERALIST" (PAPERS)? $800

$1000   WHO IS DANIEL SHAYS? $1000

DOUBLE JEOPARDY!

MOVIES ABOUT THE MOVIES

THIS GENE KELLY MUSICAL TAKES PLACE IN A HOLLYWOOD MAKING THE ADJUSTMENT TO TALKIES	**$200**	WHAT IS
HE DIRECTED "8½", A MOVIE ABOUT A MOVIE DIRECTOR	**$400**	WHO IS
IN THIS 1941 PRESTON STURGES FILM, A DIRECTOR SETS OUT TO RESEARCH POVERTY WITH ONLY A DIME IN HIS POCKET	**$600**	WHAT IS
JOHN TURTURRO PLAYED THIS TITLE SCREENWRITER IN A 1991 COEN BROTHERS FILM	**$800**	WHO IS
THE 1998 FILM "GODS AND MONSTERS" PRESENTS THE LAST DAYS OF THIS DIRECTOR OF "FRANKENSTEIN"	**$1000**	WHO IS

DOUBLE JEOPARDY!

MOVIES ABOUT THE MOVIES

$200   WHAT IS "SINGIN' IN THE RAIN"? $200

$400   WHO IS FEDERICO FELLINI? $400

$600   WHAT IS "SULLIVAN'S TRAVELS"? $600

$800   WHO IS BARTON FINK? $800

$1000   WHO IS JAMES WHALE? $1000

DOUBLE JEOPARDY!

THAT'S WHAT THEY SAID

AFTER HER ELECTION, THIS BRITISH PRIME MINISTER SAID THAT SHE OWED "EVERY-THING TO MY FATHER"	$200	WHO IS
THIS AUTHOR'S MR. BUMBLE DECLARED THAT "THE LAW IS A ASS, A IDIOT"	$400	WHO IS
IN 1803 JACQUES DELILLE WROTE, "FATE CHOOSES OUR RELATIVES, WE CHOOSE" THESE	$600	WHAT ARE
"WHEN THE ONE GREAT SCORER COMES TO WRITE AGAINST YOUR NAME, HE MARKS—NOT THAT YOU WON OR LOST—BUT" THIS	$800	WHAT IS
IN HIS 1918 POEM "PRAIRIE", HE WROTE "I TELL YOU THE PAST IS A BUCKET OF ASHES"	$1000	WHO IS

DOUBLE JEOPARDY!

THAT'S WHAT THEY SAID

$200	WHO IS MARGARET THATCHER?	$200
$400	WHO IS CHARLES DICKENS?	$400
$600	WHAT ARE "OUR FRIENDS"?	$600
$800	WHAT IS "HOW YOU PLAYED THE GAME"?	$800
$1000	WHO IS CARL SANDBURG?	$1000

DOUBLE JEOPARDY!

THE FATHERS OF ...

"THE FATHER OF FROZEN FOODS", HE BECAME A CONSULTANT TO GENERAL FOODS	$200	WHO IS
BEFORE HE WAS "THE FATHER OF BASKETBALL", HE WAS A STAR LACROSSE PLAYER	$400	WHO IS
WE'LL TAKE AN OATH THAT HE'S "THE FATHER OF MEDICINE"	$600	WHO IS
HE MADE LIFE MISERABLE FOR BOSS TWEED AS "THE FATHER OF AMERICAN POLITICAL CARTOONISTS"	$800	WHO IS
AS YOU MIGHT EXPECT, A MAN WITH THIS COMMON LAST NAME WAS "THE FATHER OF THE TOMMY GUN"	$1000	WHAT IS

DOUBLE JEOPARDY!

THE FATHERS OF ...

$200 — WHO IS CLARENCE BIRDSEYE? — $200

$400 — WHO IS JAMES NAISMITH? — $400

$600 — WHO IS HIPPOCRATES? — $600

$800 — WHO IS THOMAS NAST? — $800

$1000 — WHAT IS THOMPSON? — $1000

DOUBLE JEOPARDY!

WORLD CAPITALS

WHEN IT GETS HOT IN THIS SOUTH AMERICAN COUNTRY, YOU MAY WANT TO DO THE FULL MONTEVIDEO	**$200**	WHAT IS
THE HEADQUARTERS OF THE ORGANIZATION OF AFRICAN UNITY ARE IN THIS ETHIOPIAN CAPITAL	**$400**	WHAT IS
THIS COUNTRY'S CAPITAL, VIENTIANE, IS LOCATED ON THE MEKONG RIVER	**$600**	WHAT IS
TIRANE, NOT TO BE CONFUSED WITH TEHRAN, IS THE CAPITAL OF THIS BALKAN NATION	**$800**	WHAT IS
IN MAY 2000 GEORGE SPEIGHT LED A COUP IN SUVA, THIS COUNTRY'S CAPITAL	**$1000**	WHAT IS

DOUBLE JEOPARDY!

WORLD CAPITALS

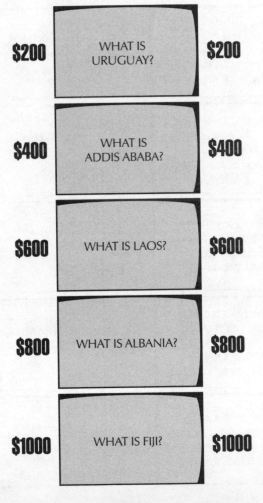

$200   WHAT IS URUGUAY? $200

$400   WHAT IS ADDIS ABABA? $400

$600   WHAT IS LAOS? $600

$800   WHAT IS ALBANIA? $800

$1000   WHAT IS FIJI? $1000

FINAL JEOPARDY!
BUSINESS MACHINES

THIS TYPE OF MACHINE,
IN THE NEWS IN 1987,
WAS DEVELOPED IN THE
'70s FROM A NOODLE-
MAKING DEVICE

WHAT IS

FINAL JEOPARDY!

BUSINESS MACHINES

WHAT IS A
(PAPER) SHREDDER?

JEOPARDY!

1820s AMERICA

ON OCT. 26, 1825 THE SENECA CHIEF LEFT BUFFALO & BECAME THE FIRST BOAT TO TRAVEL THIS WATER-WAY'S ENTIRE LENGTH	**$100**	WHAT IS
DISCOVERED IN 1806, THIS COLORADO PEAK WAS FIRST CLIMBED IN 1820 BY 3 MEMBERS OF MAJOR LONG'S EXPEDITION	**$200**	WHAT IS
ON JUNE 17, 1825 THIS FRENCHMAN LAID THE CORNERSTONE OF THE BUNKER HILL MONUMENT	**$300**	WHO IS
IN 1821 IT ENTERED THE UNION AS A SLAVE STATE WITH THOMAS HART BENTON REPRE-SENTING IT IN THE SENATE	**$400**	WHAT IS
IN HIS 1829 MESSAGE TO CONGRESS, ANDREW JACKSON QUESTIONED THE CONSTITUTIONALITY OF THIS INSTITUTION	**$500**	WHAT IS

JEOPARDY!

1820s AMERICA

$100	WHAT IS THE ERIE CANAL?	**$100**
$200	WHAT IS PIKES PEAK?	**$200**
$300	WHO IS THE MARQUIS DE LAFAYETTE?	**$300**
$400	WHAT IS MISSOURI?	**$400**
$500	WHAT IS THE BANK OF THE UNITED STATES?	**$500**

JEOPARDY!™

"SMALL" TIME

IN 1979 THE WORLD HEALTH ORGANIZATION MARKED THE DISAPPEARANCE OF THIS VIRAL DISEASE FROM THE EARTH	**$100**	WHAT IS
THIS FEDERAL LOAN-ASSISTANCE AGENCY LOCATED IN WASHINGTON, D.C. IS KNOWN AS THE SBA FOR SHORT	**$200**	WHAT IS
IT'S WHAT YOU SAY ON FINDING OUT THAT A NEW ACQUAINTANCE WENT TO COLLEGE WITH YOUR UNCLE'S DOCTOR'S COUSIN	**$300**	WHAT IS
1998 FILM ABOUT TOY ACTION FIGURES TURNED MENACING	**$400**	WHAT IS
THE NATIONAL WEATHER SERVICE ISSUES SAILORS THESE "ADVISORIES" WHEN WINDS ARE BETWEEN 18 & 33 KNOTS	**$500**	WHAT IS

JEOPARDY!

"SMALL" TIME

$100 WHAT IS SMALLPOX? **$100**

$200 WHAT IS THE SMALL BUSINESS ADMINISTRATION? **$200**

$300 WHAT IS "SMALL WORLD!"? **$300**

$400 WHAT IS "SMALL SOLDIERS"? **$400**

$500 WHAT IS A SMALL CRAFT ADVISORY? **$500**

JEOPARDY!

GANGSTERS

Clue	Value	Response
HE'S QUOTED AS SAYING, "THEY'VE HUNG EVERYTHING ON ME BUT THE CHICAGO FIRE"	$100	WHO IS
ARNOLD "THE BRAIN" ROTHSTEIN WAS ACCUSED OF MASTERMINDING THE BIG FIX OF THIS IN 1919; IT WASN'T PROVED	$200	WHAT IS
HIS BROTHER BUCK WAS PART OF HIS GANG, AS WAS HIS MOLL BONNIE	$300	WHO IS
HIS FATEFUL JULY 22, 1934 NIGHT AT CHICAGO'S BIOGRAPH THEATER MIGHT BE FEATURED ON "BIOGRAPHY"	$400	WHO IS
BRIBES FROM BIG BILL DWYER TURNED MEMBERS OF THIS ARMED SERVICE INTO RUM-RUNNERS	$500	WHO ARE

JEOPARDY!

GANGSTERS

$100	WHO IS AL CAPONE?	$100
$200	WHAT IS THE WORLD SERIES?	$200
$300	WHO IS CLYDE BARROW?	$300
$400	WHO IS JOHN DILLINGER?	$400
$500	WHO ARE THE U.S. COAST GUARD?	$500

JEOPARDY!

1990s NONFICTION

NOTABLE ONES INCLUDE McCULLOUGH'S OF TRUMAN, BERG'S OF LINDBERGH & JACK MILES' OF GOD	**$100**	WHAT ARE
THIS NEWS PERSON-ALITY'S "AMERICA" TOLD OF HIS 12 FAVORITE PLACES FOUND "ON THE ROAD"	**$200**	WHO IS
SEYMOUR HERSH'S 1997 JFK EXPOSE WAS TITLED "THE DARK SIDE OF" THIS	**$300**	WHAT IS
THIS AUTHOR WAS BORN IN BROOKLYN BUT, AS "ANGELA'S ASHES" TELLS, GREW UP IN IRELAND	**$400**	WHO IS
A MOSCOW MAUSOLEUM, OR THE TITLE OF DAVID REMNICK'S BOOK ON "THE LAST DAYS OF THE SOVIET EMPIRE"	**$500**	WHAT IS

JEOPARDY!

1990s NONFICTION

$100	WHAT ARE BIOGRAPHIES?	**$100**
$200	WHO IS CHARLES KURALT?	**$200**
$300	WHAT IS "CAMELOT"?	**$300**
$400	WHO IS FRANK McCOURT?	**$400**
$500	WHAT IS LENIN'S TOMB?	**$500**

JEOPARDY!

BOXING TERMS

Clue	Value	Response
NEW TO THE SPORT? LET ME SHOW YOU THESE; THEY'RE STRUNG AROUND THE RING	**$100**	WHAT ARE
A PUNCH DELIVERED "BELOW" IT IS A FOUL (& MAY CAUSE YOU TO LOSE IT)	**$200**	WHAT IS
THE MOST IMPORTANT BOUT ON THE CARD; BARBRA STREISAND SANG ABOUT ONE	**$300**	WHAT IS
FOR THE COUNT, THE STANDING BOXER MUST RETIRE TO ONE OF THESE	**$400**	WHAT IS
IN 1982 NEVADA MADE THIS COUNT MANDATORY IN CASE OF A KNOCKDOWN	**$500**	WHAT IS

165

JEOPARDY!

BOXING TERMS

$100	WHAT ARE THE ROPES?	**$100**
$200	WHAT IS THE BELT?	**$200**
$300	WHAT IS "THE MAIN EVENT"?	**$300**
$400	WHAT IS A NEUTRAL CORNER?	**$400**
$500	WHAT IS AN (STANDING) EIGHT COUNT?	**$500**

JEOPARDY!

CHARLES DARWIN

CHARLES & THIS AMERICAN PRESIDENT WERE BORN ON THE SAME DAY, FEBRUARY 12, 1809; CHARLES LIVED MUCH LONGER	**$100**	WHO IS
YOUNG CHARLES HAD JOHN EDMONSTONE TEACH HIM THIS ART WHOSE MOTTO MAY BE "GET STUFFED"	**$200**	WHAT IS
IT WAS DARWIN'S FAVORITE PROFESSOR WHO RECOMMENDED HIM FOR THE NATURALIST POST ABOARD THIS SHIP	**$300**	WHAT IS
A GALAPAGOS GOVERNOR TOLD DARWIN HE COULD LOOK AT ONE OF THESE GIANT CREATURES & IDENTIFY ITS ISLAND	**$400**	WHAT ARE
THE GRANDFATHER OF THIS "BRAVE NEW WORLD" AUTHOR WAS KNOWN AS "DARWIN'S BULLDOG"	**$500**	WHO IS

JEOPARDY!

CHARLES DARWIN

$100	WHO IS ABRAHAM LINCOLN?
$200	WHAT IS TAXIDERMY?
$300	WHAT IS THE BEAGLE?
$400	WHAT ARE TORTOISES?
$500	WHO IS ALDOUS HUXLEY?

DOUBLE JEOPARDY!

MEET THE FLINTSTONES

"THE FLINTSTONES" WAS MODELED ON THIS JACKIE GLEASON SERIES	**$200**	WHAT IS
IN THE 1993 PRIME-TIME SPECIAL "I YABBA-DABBA DO!", THESE 2 KIDS GOT MARRIED	**$400**	WHO ARE
IN 1996, AFTER YEARS OF EXCLUSION & A NATIONAL VOTE, SHE JOINED THE REST OF THE GANG AS A FLINTSTONE VITAMIN	**$600**	WHO IS
KRISTEN JOHNSTON PLAYED WILMA IN THE 2000 FILM "THE FLINTSTONES IN VIVA" THIS PLACE	**$800**	WHAT IS
"THE FLINTSTONES" THEME IS BASED ON THE CHORD CHANGES OF THIS SONG; "WHO COULD ASK FOR ANYTHING MORE?"	**$1000**	WHAT IS

DOUBLE JEOPARDY!

MEET THE FLINTSTONES

$200	WHAT IS "THE HONEYMOONERS"?	**$200**
$400	WHO ARE PEBBLES & BAMM-BAMM?	**$400**
$600	WHO IS BETTY (RUBBLE)?	**$600**
$800	WHAT IS ROCK VEGAS?	**$800**
$1000	WHAT IS "I GOT RHYTHM"?	**$1000**

DOUBLE JEOPARDY!

GEOGRAPHY

MANY RESIDENTS OF THIS SPRAWLING VALLEY THAT INCLUDES NORTH HOLLYWOOD WANT TO SECEDE FROM LOS ANGELES	**$200**	WHAT IS
MOST OF THE RESIDENTS OF THIS SMALL ISLAND CITY-STATE OFF THE MALAY PENINSULA ARE CHINESE	**$400**	WHAT IS
THE SHRINE OF FATIMA IS IN THIS COUNTRY'S CITY OF QOM, NOT FAR FROM TEHRAN	**$600**	WHAT IS
QUEENSLAND & VICTORIA ARE 2 OF THIS COUNTRY'S STATES	**$800**	WHAT IS
THIS "STAN" IS WEDGED IN AMONG TURKMEN-ISTAN, KAZAKHSTAN, TAJIKISTAN & KYRGYZSTAN	**$1000**	WHAT IS

DOUBLE JEOPARDY!

GEOGRAPHY

$200	WHAT IS THE SAN FERNANDO VALLEY?	**$200**
$400	WHAT IS SINGAPORE?	**$400**
$600	WHAT IS IRAN?	**$600**
$800	WHAT IS AUSTRALIA?	**$800**
$1000	WHAT IS UZBEKISTAN?	**$1000**

DOUBLE JEOPARDY!

GOING TO THE DOGE

NICKNAME OF THE BRIDGE ANTONIO CONTINO BUILT AROUND 1600; IT CONNECTS THE PRISON & THE DOGE'S PALACE	$200	WHAT IS
DOGE ENRICO DANDOLO ISSUED THESE, CALLED GROSSOS, WITH HIS PICTURE ON THEM	$400	WHAT ARE
14th CENTURY DOGE MARINO FALIERO WAS THE SUBJECT OF A TRAGEDY BY THIS "DON JUAN" POET	$600	WHO IS
SIMONE BOCCANEGRA WAS THE FIRST DOGE OF THIS CITY, HOME TO COLUMBUS	$800	WHAT IS
THIS CATHEDRAL IN VENICE WAS ORIGINALLY A PRIVATE CHAPEL OF THE DOGES	$1000	WHAT IS

DOUBLE JEOPARDY!

GOING TO THE DOGE

$200	WHAT IS THE BRIDGE OF SIGHS?
$400	WHAT ARE (SILVER) COINS?
$600	WHO IS LORD BYRON?
$800	WHAT IS GENOA?
$1000	WHAT IS SAINT MARK'S CATHEDRAL?

DOUBLE JEOPARDY!

WEDDINGS

FOR A VEGAS CERE-MONY, YOU MAY WANT SOMEONE DRESSED AS THIS MAN WHO SANG "WEAR MY RING AROUND YOUR NECK"	**$200**	WHO IS
IN A PROTESTANT WEDDING CEREMONY, IT'S THE ROLE OF THE FATHER OF THE BRIDE	**$400**	WHAT IS
LUKE & LAURA'S 1981 TV WEDDING WAS CRASHED BY HELENA CASSADINE, PLAYED BY THIS SUPERSTAR	**$600**	WHO IS
THE 2-MONTH SALARY BENCHMARK FOR A RING-BUYING BUDGET WAS SET BY THIS DIAMOND MINING COMPANY IN THE 1980s	**$800**	WHAT IS
BORN IN 1809, THIS GERMAN COMPOSER WAS 17 WHEN HE BEGAN WORK ON HIS "WEDDING MARCH"	**$1000**	WHO IS

DOUBLE JEOPARDY!

WEDDINGS

$200   WHO IS ELVIS PRESLEY? $200

$400   WHAT IS TO GIVE THE BRIDE AWAY? $400

$600   WHO IS ELIZABETH TAYLOR? $600

$800   WHAT IS DE BEERS? $800

$1000   WHO IS FELIX MENDELSSOHN? $1000

DOUBLE JEOPARDY!

SAY CHEESE!

HIS "POOR RICHARD'S ALMANAC" SAYS THAT "CHEESE AND SALT MEAT SHOULD BE SPARINGLY EAT"	**$200**	WHO IS
"MANY'S THE LONG NIGHT I'VE DREAMED OF CHEESE—TOASTED, MOSTLY", THIS AUTHOR WROTE IN "TREASURE ISLAND"	**$400**	WHO IS
THIS FRENCH PRESIDENT ASKED HOW ONE COULD BE EXPECTED TO GOVERN A COUNTRY THAT HAS "265 KINDS OF CHEESE?"	**$600**	WHO IS
THIS BROWNING WORK SAYS, "RATS! THEY FOUGHT THE DOGS AND KILLED THE CATS . . . AND ATE THE CHEESES OUT OF THE VATS"	**$800**	WHAT IS
IN HIS INTRODUCTION TO "A TALE OF A TUB", THIS IRISH-BORN SATIRIST SAYS THAT WISDOM "IS A CHEESE"	**$1000**	WHO IS

DOUBLE JEOPARDY!

SAY CHEESE!

$200	WHO IS BENJAMIN FRANKLIN?	**$200**
$400	WHO IS ROBERT LOUIS STEVENSON?	**$400**
$600	WHO IS CHARLES DE GAULLE?	**$600**
$800	WHAT IS "THE PIED PIPER (OF HAMELIN)"?	**$800**
$1000	WHO IS JONATHAN SWIFT?	**$1000**

DOUBLE JEOPARDY!

THEY REST IN RHODE ISLAND

SWAN POINT CEMETERY IS HOME TO ELISHA HUNT RHODES, WHOSE DIARY KEN BURNS USED IN A SHOW ON THIS SUBJECT	**$200**	WHAT IS
NICHOLAS COLASANTO, WHO WAS BEHIND THE BAR AS COACH ON THIS SITCOM, IS IN A CRANSTON, R.I. CEMETERY	**$400**	WHAT IS
LAST NAME OF THE 2 NAVAL BROTHERS, OLIVER & MATTHEW, WHO LIE IN ISLAND CEMETERY	**$600**	WHAT IS
THIS FOUNDER OF RHODE ISLAND HAS HIS OWN MEMORIAL IN PROVIDENCE	**$800**	WHO IS
THIS WRITER WHO CREATED CTHULHU WAS BORN, BRED & BURIED IN RHODE ISLAND	**$1000**	WHO IS

DOUBLE JEOPARDY!

THEY REST IN RHODE ISLAND

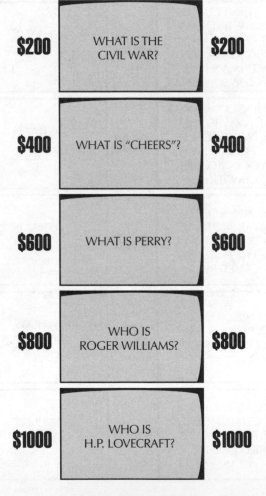

$200 — WHAT IS THE CIVIL WAR? — $200

$400 — WHAT IS "CHEERS"? — $400

$600 — WHAT IS PERRY? — $600

$800 — WHO IS ROGER WILLIAMS? — $800

$1000 — WHO IS H.P. LOVECRAFT? — $1000

FINAL JEOPARDY!

STATUES

ITS FACE WAS MODELED ON THE FEATURES OF AUGUSTE-CHARLOTTE BARTHOLDI

WHAT IS

FINAL JEOPARDY!

STATUES

WHAT IS THE
STATUE OF LIBERTY?

JEOPARDY!

NAME THE DECADE

PAUL REVERE TAKES A MIDNIGHT RIDE & WARNS THAT "THE BRITISH ARE COMING"	$100	WHAT ARE
WALTER MONDALE IS NOMINATED FOR PRESIDENT OF THE UNITED STATES	$200	WHAT ARE
THE 19th AMENDMENT IS RATIFIED; WOMEN CAN NOW VOTE!	$300	WHAT ARE
GOOD HEAVENS! ASTRONOMER CLYDE TOMBAUGH DISCOVERS PLUTO	$400	WHAT ARE
THE MAINE MYSTERI-OUSLY BLOWS UP IN HAVANA HARBOR	$500	WHAT ARE

JEOPARDY!

NAME THE DECADE

$100 WHAT ARE THE 1770s? **$100**

$200 WHAT ARE THE 1980s? **$200**

$300 WHAT ARE THE 1920s? **$300**

$400 WHAT ARE THE 1930s? **$400**

$500 WHAT ARE THE 1890s? **$500**

JEOPARDY!

CINCINNATI

CINCINNATI'S ORIGINAL FOOTBALL TEAM CALLED THIS DIDN'T GET ITS NAME FROM THE TIGER, BUT FROM SOLDIERS IN INDIA	**$100**	WHAT ARE
THE SCULPTURE "GENIUS OF WATER" CROWNS ONE OF THESE STRUCTURES AT THE HEART OF CINCINNATI'S DOWNTOWN	**$200**	WHAT IS
AT OKTOBERFEST 1994, 48,000 CINCINNATIANS FLAPPED THEIR ELBOWS LIKE WINGS IN THIS DANCE	**$300**	WHAT IS
THE CONVENTION CENTER IS NAMED FOR DR. ALBERT SABIN, BEST KNOWN FOR DEVELOPING THIS IN CINCI IN THE '50s	**$400**	WHAT IS
THE GREATER CINCINNATI AIRPORT IS ACTUALLY ACROSS THE OHIO RIVER IN THIS STATE	**$500**	WHAT IS

JEOPARDY!

CINCINNATI

$100	WHAT ARE THE BENGALS?	**$100**
$200	WHAT IS A FOUNTAIN?	**$200**
$300	WHAT IS THE CHICKEN DANCE?	**$300**
$400	WHAT IS (ORAL) POLIO VACCINE?	**$400**
$500	WHAT IS KENTUCKY?	**$500**

JEOPARDY!

G.G.'s

SHE WAS ONLY IN HER 30s WHEN SHE RETIRED FROM FILM AFTER THE RELEASE OF "TWO-FACED WOMAN" IN 1941	$100	WHO IS
THIS COMPOSER'S "PORGY AND BESS" IS PERHAPS THE MOST POPULAR OPERA EVER WRITTEN BY AN AMERICAN	$200	WHO IS
HE PROVIDED LIVE COVERAGE OF THE SUMMER OLYMPICS FROM ATLANTA, WHILE BROTHER BRYANT COVERED EVENTS IN NAGANO	$300	WHO IS
HER DISCO HIT "I WILL SURVIVE" BECAME AN ANTHEM FOR MANY WOMEN & IS STILL POPULAR TODAY	$400	WHO IS
NORMAN MAILER WROTE ABOUT THE LIFE & DEATH OF THIS CONVICTED KILLER IN HIS BOOK "THE EXECUTIONER'S SONG"	$500	WHO IS

JEOPARDY!

G.G.'s

$100   WHO IS GRETA GARBO?   **$100**

$200   WHO IS GEORGE GERSHWIN?   **$200**

$300   WHO IS GREG GUMBEL?   **$300**

$400   WHO IS GLORIA GAYNOR?   **$400**

$500   WHO IS GARY GILMORE?   **$500**

JEOPARDY!

ONE WORD MISSING

Clue	Value	Response
OH, TO BE IN ___ , / NOW THAT APRIL'S THERE	**$100**	WHAT IS
HAD WE BUT ___ ENOUGH, AND TIME, / THIS COYNESS, LADY, WERE NO CRIME	**$200**	WHAT IS
AN ___ MAN'S THE NOBLEST WORK OF GOD	**$300**	WHAT IS
I SHOULD HAVE BEEN A PAIR OF RAGGED ___ / SCUTTLING ACROSS THE FLOORS OF SILENT SEAS	**$400**	WHAT IS
MADE WEAK BY TIME AND FATE, BUT STRONG IN WILL / TO STRIVE, TO SEEK, TO FIND AND NOT TO ___	**$500**	WHAT IS

JEOPARDY!

ONE WORD MISSING

$100   WHAT IS ENGLAND? $100

$200   WHAT IS WORLD? $200

$300   WHAT IS HONEST? $300

$400   WHAT IS CLAWS? $400

$500   WHAT IS YIELD? $500

JEOPARDY!

HAIR CARE

A DAB OF PHYTO-SPECIFIC RELAXER MIGHT HAVE CONTROLLED THIS STANDOUT ON ALFALFA'S HEAD	**$100**	WHAT IS
THE BOBBY PIN WAS INTRODUCED IN THIS DECADE KNOWN FOR ITS BOBBED HAIR CRAZE	**$200**	WHAT ARE
IN 1954 THE "NO MORE TEARS" FORMULA OF THIS PRODUCT WAS INTRODUCED	**$300**	WHAT IS
AN ARCHIVE OF THIS SHAMPOO'S "GIRLS", INCLUDING BROOKE & CYBILL, IS HOUSED AT THE SMITHSONIAN	**$400**	WHAT IS
SALON HAIR CARE LINE HEADED & MODELED BY JOHN PAUL DeJORIA	**$500**	WHAT IS

JEOPARDY!

HAIR CARE

$100   WHAT IS A COWLICK? $100

$200   WHAT ARE THE 1920s? $200

$300   WHAT IS (JOHNSON &) JOHNSON'S BABY SHAMPOO? $300

$400   WHAT IS BRECK? $400

$500   WHAT IS PAUL MITCHELL? $500

JEOPARDY!

CHILDREN'S LITERATURE

IN A FOLKTALE, THIS YUMMY "MAN" RUNS AWAY AFTER HE IS BAKED & IS LATER EATEN BY A SLY FOX	**$100**	WHO IS
MOWGLI IS THE MAIN CHARACTER OF THESE IMAGINATIVE RUDYARD KIPLING "BOOKS"	**$200**	WHAT ARE
IN THIS HANS CHRISTIAN ANDERSEN STORY, A CHILD OBSERVES, "HE HAS GOT NOTHING ON AT ALL!"	**$300**	WHAT IS
FERDINAND, THIS TYPE OF ANIMAL, JUST LIKES TO SIT & SMELL THE FLOWERS	**$400**	WHAT IS
IN A 1970 JUDY BLUME BOOK, THIS TITLE CHARACTER ASKED, "ARE YOU THERE GOD?"	**$500**	WHO IS

JEOPARDY!™

CHILDREN'S LITERATURE

$100 WHO IS THE GINGERBREAD MAN? **$100**

$200 WHAT ARE THE JUNGLE BOOKS? **$200**

$300 WHAT IS "THE EMPEROR'S NEW CLOTHES"? **$300**

$400 WHAT IS A BULL? **$400**

$500 WHO IS MARGARET (SIMON)? **$500**

DOUBLE JEOPARDY!

OSCAR-WINNING ROLES

HE WAS MORE THAN A CONTENDER AS THE BRAVE & SOMEWHAT DIM TERRY MALLOY	$200	WHO IS
HE WON FOR PLAYING A SUBURBAN DAD COMING TO LIFE IN "AMERICAN BEAUTY"	$400	WHO IS
BOXER PLAYED BY ROBERT DE NIRO IN "RAGING BULL"	$600	WHO IS
HE WON FOR PLAYING BLIND LT. COL. FRANK SLADE (RET.)	$800	WHO IS
GWYNETH PALTROW'S "SHAKESPEARE IN LOVE" CHARACTER SHARED THIS FIRST NAME WITH THE HEROINE OF "TWELFTH NIGHT"	$1000	WHAT IS

DOUBLE JEOPARDY!

OSCAR-WINNING ROLES

$200	WHO IS MARLON BRANDO?	**$200**
$400	WHO IS KEVIN SPACEY?	**$400**
$600	WHO IS JAKE LA MOTTA?	**$600**
$800	WHO IS AL PACINO?	**$800**
$1000	WHAT IS VIOLA?	**$1000**

DOUBLE JEOPARDY!

THE BLUE & THE GRAY

Clue	Value	Response
DANIEL HOUGH, THE CIVIL WAR'S FIRST FATALITY, DIED NOT IN BATTLE BUT IN AN ACCIDENT AT THIS FORT	$200	WHAT IS
THE SIEGE OF VICKS-BURG IN 1863 GAVE THE UNION CONTROL OF THIS RIVER	$400	WHAT IS
LESS THAN A MONTH AFTER GRADUATING LAST IN HIS CLASS FROM WEST POINT, HE MADE HIS FIRST STAND AT BULL RUN	$600	WHO IS
ROBERT E. LEE LOST NEARLY A QUARTER OF HIS TROOPS IN THIS MARYLAND BATTLE ALSO CALLED SHARPSBURG	$800	WHAT IS
THOUGH RELIEVED AS UNION ARMY CHIEF IN MARCH 1862, HE CONTINUED TO LEAD THE ARMY OF THE POTOMAC UNTIL NOVEMBER	$1000	WHO IS

DOUBLE JEOPARDY!

THE BLUE & THE GRAY

$200 | WHAT IS FORT SUMTER? | $200

$400 | WHAT IS THE MISSISSIPPI? | $400

$600 | WHO IS GEORGE CUSTER? | $600

$800 | WHAT IS ANTIETAM? | $800

$1000 | WHO IS GEORGE McCLELLAN? | $1000

DOUBLE JEOPARDY!

FASHION FOLKS

BEGUN IN 1913 & STILL IN OPERATION, THIS FASHION HOUSE "DE COCO" WAS CLOSED DOWN DURING WWII	**$200**	WHAT IS
THE MUCH TALKED-ABOUT FASHION DE-SIGN FIRM OF THIS MAN HAS BEEN HIS "OBSES-SION" SINCE 1968	**$400**	WHO IS
THIS HIP DESIGNER FOR BOYS & "GIRL"S DESCRIBES THE AMERICAN STYLE OF HIS LINE AS "GOOD, CLEAN FUN"	**$600**	WHO IS
A FAMOUS REPTILIAN LOGO BELONGS TO THE DESIGN HOUSE BEGUN BY THIS TENNIS PLAYER	**$800**	WHO IS
AS SEEN ON RICHARD GERE IN "AMERICAN GIGOLO", SEXY SUITS FOR MEN WERE EARLY SUCCESSES FOR THIS FASHION LINE	**$1000**	WHAT IS

DOUBLE JEOPARDY!

FASHION FOLKS

$200	WHAT IS CHANEL?	**$200**
$400	WHO IS CALVIN KLEIN?	**$400**
$600	WHO IS TOMMY HILFIGER?	**$600**
$800	WHO IS RENE LACOSTE?	**$800**
$1000	WHAT IS ARMANI?	**$1000**

DOUBLE JEOPARDY!

"A" PLUS

FIRST NAME OF TV's McBEAL	$200	WHO IS
THIS WORD FOR A PAYMENT TO A FORMER SPOUSE IS FROM THE LATIN FOR "SUS-TENANCE" OR "NOURISHMENT"	$400	WHAT IS
IN A 1992 SONG TITLE, IT DESCRIBES BILLY RAY CYRUS' HEART	$600	WI IAT IS
A 2000 BOOK BY MOUNTAINEER REINHOLD MESSNER CLAIMS TO SOLVE THE MYSTERY OF THIS "SNOWMAN"	$800	WHAT IS
A CEREBRAL HEMORRHAGE, OR A FIT OF RAGE	$1000	WHAT IS

DOUBLE JEOPARDY!

"A" PLUS

$200	WHO IS ALLY?	**$200**
$400	WHAT IS ALIMONY?	**$400**
$600	WHAT IS ACHY BREAKY?	**$600**
$800	WHAT IS THE ABOMINABLE (SNOWMAN)?	**$800**
$1000	WHAT IS APOPLEXY?	**$1000**

DOUBLE JEOPARDY!

CHEMISTRY

Clue	Value	Response
YOU CAN ISOLATE ABOUT 1 GRAM OF THIS ELEMENT, Ra, OUT OF SEVERAL TONS OF PITCHBLENDE	$200	WHAT IS
IN THE 1700s GEORG ERNST STAHL COINED THE PHLOGISTON THEORY, THAT A FORM OF BURNING CAUSED THIS ON IRON	$400	WHAT IS
A FREE RADICAL IS AN ATOM OR MOLECULE THAT HAS AN ODD NUMBER OF THESE	$600	WHAT ARE
LITHIUM REACTS WITH THIS COMMON SUB-STANCE TO FORM LITHIUM HYDROXIDE	$800	WHAT IS
BROMINE & CHLORINE ARE IN A GROUP OF ELEMENTS KNOWN BY THIS NAME, FROM THE GREEK FOR "SALT-FORMING"	$1000	WHAT ARE

DOUBLE JEOPARDY!

CHEMISTRY

$200	WHAT IS RADIUM?	**$200**
$400	WHAT IS RUST?	**$400**
$600	WHAT ARE ELECTRONS?	**$600**
$800	WHAT IS WATER?	**$800**
$1000	WHAT ARE HALOGENS?	**$1000**

DOUBLE JEOPARDY!

BORN ON THE THIRD OF JULY

THIS "YANKEE DOODLE DANDY" COMPOSER WAS ACTUALLY BORN ON JULY 3 IN 1878	**$200**	WHO IS
"ROSENCRANTZ AND GUILDENSTERN ARE DEAD" IS A CLASSIC BY THIS JULY 3-BORN BRITISH PLAYWRIGHT	**$400**	WHO IS
BORN JULY 3, 1883 IN PRAGUE, THIS AUTHOR DIED AFTER A "TRIAL" WITH TB IN AN AUSTRIAN SANITARIUM JUNE 3, 1924	**$600**	WHO IS
BORN JULY 3, 1951, AT AGE 19 HE BECAME HAITI'S "PRESIDENT FOR LIFE"; WHY, HE WAS JUST A "BABY"	**$800**	WHO IS
ABOUT 200 YEARS BEFORE "JAWS", THIS AMERICAN PAINTER BORN JULY 3, 1738 PAINTED "WATSON AND THE SHARK"	**$1000**	WHO IS

DOUBLE JEOPARDY!

BORN ON THE THIRD OF JULY

$200   WHO IS GEORGE M. COHAN? $200

$400   WHO IS TOM STOPPARD? $400

$600   WHO IS FRANZ KAFKA? $600

$800   WHO IS JEAN-CLAUDE "BABY DOC" DUVALIER? $800

$1000   WHO IS JOHN SINGLETON COPLEY? $1000

FINAL JEOPARDY!

CONTEMPORARY AMERICANS

THEY WERE THE 2 MAIN
FOUNDERS OF MICROSOFT

WHO ARE

FINAL JEOPARDY!

CONTEMPORARY AMERICANS

WHO ARE
BILL GATES & PAUL ALLEN?

JEOPARDY!

OFFICIAL STATE STUFF

THIS "FIRST STATE" HAS THE MOTTO "LIBERTY AND INDEPENDENCE"	**$100**	WHAT IS
THIS "CRAZY" CREATURE IS MINNESOTA'S STATE BIRD	**$200**	WHAT IS
THIS TREE THAT SOUNDS LIKE IT PRODUCES FABRIC IS WYOMING'S STATE TREE	**$300**	WHAT IS
MISSOURI'S STATE ONE OF THESE IS THE HAWTHORN	**$400**	WHAT IS
SOUTH DAKOTA'S STATE FISH IS THIS ONE THAT LOOKS AT YOU FUNNY	**$500**	WHAT IS

JEOPARDY!

OFFICIAL STATE STUFF

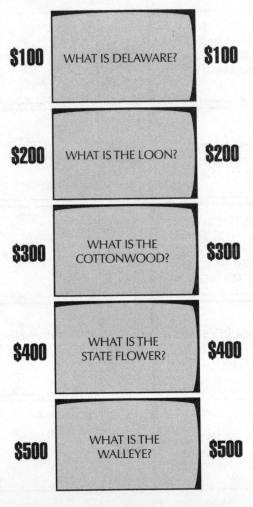

$100   WHAT IS DELAWARE? $100

$200   WHAT IS THE LOON? $200

$300   WHAT IS THE COTTONWOOD? $300

$400   WHAT IS THE STATE FLOWER? $400

$500   WHAT IS THE WALLEYE? $500

JEOPARDY!

PIRATES

AMERICAN FORCES WON THIS JANUARY 1815 BATTLE WITH THE HELP OF PIRATES LED BY JEAN LAFFITE	**$100**	WHAT IS
A TYPE OF OLDSMOBILE SHARES ITS NAME WITH THIS KIND OF SWORD NO SELF-RESPECTING PIRATE WOULD BE WITHOUT	**$200**	WHAT IS
PIRATES OFFICIALLY LICENSED TO ATTACK ENEMY SHIPS DURING WARTIME WERE KNOWN BY THIS "SECRETIVE" NAME	**$300**	WHAT ARE
THIS "COLORFUL" PIRATE WAS PAID BY THE BRITISH TO ATTACK SPANISH SHIPS IN THE EARLY 1700s	**$400**	WHO IS
FROM THE FRENCH FOR "ONE WHO CURES MEAT", IT WAS A PIRATE WHO PREYED ON SPANISH SHIPPING IN THE WEST INDIES	**$500**	WHAT IS

JEOPARDY!

PIRATES

$100	WHAT IS THE BATTLE OF NEW ORLEANS?	**$100**
$200	WHAT IS A CUTLASS?	**$200**
$300	WHAT ARE PRIVATEERS?	**$300**
$400	WHO IS BLACKBEARD?	**$400**
$500	WHAT IS A BUCCANEER?	**$500**

JEOPARDY!

ENTERTAINING CANADIANS

LAST NAME OF CANADIAN-BORN ACTRESS MEG, JENNIFER'S SISTER	**$100**	WHAT IS
MOST KNOW WILLIAM SHATNER IS CANADIAN, BUT SO IS JAMES DOOHAN, WHO PLAYED THIS "STAR TREK" ENGINEER	**$200**	WHO IS
JOSHUA JACKSON, A STAR OF THIS MASSACHUSETTS-SET WB SERIES, IS A VANCOUVER NATIVE	**$300**	WHAT IS
ON SCREEN HE'S BEEN STUDIO 54 FOUNDER STEVE RUBELL & WOULD-BE WORLD DOMINATOR DR. EVIL	**$400**	WHO IS
IN 1970 THIS TORONTO-BORN NEWSMAN BEGAN HIS 3-DECADE CAREER AT "60 MINUTES"	**$500**	WHO IS

JEOPARDY!

ENTERTAINING CANADIANS

$100	WHAT IS TILLY?	**$100**
$200	WHO IS SCOTTY?	**$200**
$300	WHAT IS "DAWSON'S CREEK"?	**$300**
$400	WHO IS MIKE MYERS?	**$400**
$500	WHO IS MORLEY SAFER?	**$500**

JEOPARDY!

WESTERN EUROPE

Clue	Value	Response
THE FRISIAN ISLANDS IN THIS SEA ARE DIVIDED AMONG GERMANY, DENMARK & THE NETHERLANDS	$100	WHAT IS
THIS 270-MILE MOUNTAIN CHAIN ONCE FORCED SPAIN & FRANCE TO TRADE BY SEA	$200	WHAT ARE
WE ASSUME THERE ARE ALSO PLENTY OF FEMALES ON THIS ISLE HALFWAY BETWEEN ENGLAND & IRELAND	$300	WHAT IS
DURING WWII THIS PALATIAL CITY SOUTH-WEST OF PARIS WAS THE SITE OF ALLIED GENERAL HEAD-QUARTERS	$400	WHAT IS
THE CELTIC SETTLEMENT LAUSONIUM, ON LAKE GENEVA, DEVELOPED INTO THIS SWISS CITY	$500	WHAT IS

JEOPARDY!

WESTERN EUROPE

$100	WHAT IS THE NORTH SEA?	**$100**
$200	WHAT ARE THE PYRENEES?	**$200**
$300	WHAT IS THE ISLE OF MAN?	**$300**
$400	WHAT IS VERSAILLES?	**$400**
$500	WHAT IS LAUSANNE?	**$500**

JEOPARDY!

DOUBLE-Z WORDS

A CHEAP, DILAPIDATED CAR, ESPECIALLY A MODEL T, IS REFERRED TO AS A TIN ONE OF THESE	**$100**	WHAT IS
IN THE TITLE OF A GOO GOO DOLLS ALBUM, IT PRECEDES "UP THE GIRL"	**$200**	WHAT IS
ON TV, IT'S THE BRAND OF BEER BREWED BY DREW CAREY & HIS FRIENDS	**$300**	WHAT IS
NICKNAME OF PRO GOLFER FRANK URBAN ZOELLER	**$400**	WHAT IS
INGRID BERGMAN STARRED IN THIS 1936 SWEDISH FILM AS WELL AS ITS HOLLYWOOD REMAKE 3 YEARS LATER	**$500**	WHAT IS

217

JEOPARDY!

DOUBLE-Z WORDS

$100   WHAT IS A LIZZIE? $100

$200   WHAT IS DIZZY? $200

$300   WHAT IS BUZZ? $300

$400   WHAT IS FUZZY? $400

$500   WHAT IS "INTERMEZZO"? $500

JEOPARDY!™

"TOM JONES"

IN BOOK 13 COUNTRY BOY TOM ARRIVES IN THIS METROPOLIS, WHERE THE CLIMACTIC ACTION TAKES PLACE	**$100**	WHAT IS
THIS AUTHOR OF THE NOVEL BASED THE HEROINE, SOPHIA, ON HIS BELOVED LATE WIFE	**$200**	WHO IS
TOM FINALLY LEARNS THE TRUE IDENTITY OF THIS PERSON; HE THOUGHT IT WAS JENNY THE MAID	**$300**	WHO IS
THE BENEVOLENT MR. ALLWORTHY & THE CRUDE MR. WESTERN HAVE THIS TITLE GIVEN TO ENGLISH COUNTRY GENTLEMEN	**$400**	WHAT IS
THIS "KUBLA KHAN" POET THOUGHT "TOM JONES" HAD 1 OF THE 3 BEST PLOTS IN ALL LITERATURE	**$500**	WHO IS

JEOPARDY!

"TOM JONES"

$100 — WHAT IS LONDON? — $100

$200 — WHO IS HENRY FIELDING? — $200

$300 — WHO IS HIS MOTHER? — $300

$400 — WHAT IS SQUIRE? — $400

$500 — WHO IS SAMUEL TAYLOR COLERIDGE? — $500

DOUBLE JEOPARDY!

BODIES OF WATER

WINDERMERE IS THE LARGEST OF THESE IN THE ENGLISH "DISTRICT" NAMED FOR THEM	**$200**	WHAT IS
BAKU IN AZERBAIJAN & ASTRAKHAN IN RUSSIA ARE PORTS ON THIS STURGEON-FILLED SEA	**$400**	WHAT IS
A 1795 LAND FRAUD CASE CONCERNED LAND NEAR THE YAZOO, A TRIBUTARY OF THIS AMERICAN RIVER	**$600**	WHAT IS
THIS BAY SEPARATING NOVA SCOTIA & NEW BRUNSWICK HAS HIGH TIDES OF UP TO 70 FEET	**$800**	WHAT IS
THE WEDDELL SEA, BORDERING THIS CONTINENT, WAS NAMED FOR JAMES WEDDELL, WHO CHARTED IT IN 1823	**$1000**	WHAT IS

DOUBLE JEOPARDY!

BODIES OF WATER

$200 WHAT IS A LAKE? **$200**

$400 WHAT IS THE CASPIAN SEA? **$400**

$600 WHAT IS THE MISSISSIPPI? **$600**

$800 WHAT IS THE BAY OF FUNDY? **$800**

$1000 WHAT IS ANTARCTICA? **$1000**

DOUBLE JEOPARDY!
LEGENDARY RHYME TIME

BUNYAN'S BARROOM FISTICUFFS	**$200**	WHAT ARE
ROBIN'S BOOTY THAT HE STOLE FROM THE RICH	**$400**	WHAT ARE
NORSE THUNDER GOD'S DAILY DUTIES	**$600**	WHAT ARE
LEGENDARY CARTHAGINIAN QUEEN'S FAITHFUL DOGS	**$800**	WHAT ARE
COUNTERPARTS OF GENTLEMEN IN THE GREEK UNDERWORLD	**$1000**	WHAT ARE

DOUBLE JEOPARDY!

LEGENDARY RHYME TIME

$200	WHAT ARE PAUL'S BRAWLS?	**$200**
$400	WHAT ARE HOOD'S GOODS?	**$400**
$600	WHAT ARE THOR'S CHORES?	**$600**
$800	WHAT ARE DIDO'S FIDOS?	**$800**
$1000	WHAT ARE HADES LADIES?	**$1000**

DOUBLE JEOPARDY!

MOVIE ACTORS & ACTRESSES

JEAN MARSH OF "UPSTAIRS/DOWN-STAIRS" PLAYED ANTONY'S WIFE OCTAVIA IN THIS TAYLOR-&-BURTON EPIC	**$200**	WHAT IS
THIS TALLER HALF OF THE "GRUMPY OLD MEN" DUO PASSED AWAY IN 2000	**$400**	WHO IS
SHIRLEY EATON PLAYED THE GILDED GLAMOR GAL IN THIS 1964 SPY CLASSIC	**$600**	WHAT IS
ORIGINALLY NAMED SUSAN STOCKARD, SHE FOUND FAME & FORTUNE WHEN SHE CO-STARRED IN "THE FORTUNE" IN 1975	**$800**	WHO IS
THIS LEADING MAN OF "SPEED II" WAS FIRST SEEN ONSCREEN IN THE FUTURISTIC FLICK "SOLARBABIES"	**$1000**	WHO IS

DOUBLE JEOPARDY!

MOVIE ACTORS & ACTRESSES

$200   WHAT IS "CLEOPATRA"? $200

$400   WHO IS WALTER MATTHAU? $400

$600   WHAT IS "GOLDFINGER"? $600

$800   WHO IS STOCKARD CHANNING? $800

$1000   WHO IS JASON PATRIC? $1000

DOUBLE JEOPARDY!

THE 1930s

Clue	Value	Response
A 6-DAY FAST BY THIS MAN IN 1932 CHANGED THE WAY THE UNTOUCHABLES IN INDIA WERE TREATED	$200	WHO IS
THE FIRST FACTORY TO MAKE THESE CARS WAS DEDICATED IN WOLFSBURG, GERMANY MAY 26, 1938	$400	WHAT ARE
IN 1931 CHEMISTS DISCOVERED A GROWTH HORMONE IN THIS GLAND	$600	WHAT IS
POPE PIUS XI's "CASTI CONNUBII" ENCYCLICAL OF 1930 WAS LARGELY A CONDEMNATION OF THIS PRACTICE	$800	WHAT IS
TOPS IN COUNTRY MUSIC IN THE '30s WERE THIS FAMILY'S A.P., SARA & MAYBELLE	$1000	WHO IS

DOUBLE JEOPARDY!

THE 1930s

$200	WHO IS MAHATMA GANDHI?	$200
$400	WHAT ARE VOLKWAGENS?	$400
$600	WHAT IS THE PITUITARY GLAND?	$600
$800	WHAT IS BIRTH CONTROL?	$800
$1000	WHO IS THE CARTER FAMILY?	$1000

DOUBLE JEOPARDY!

SCIENCE

THIS OBJECT IN A SPECTROMETER SPREADS A BEAM OF LIGHT INTO SEPARATE COLORS	**$200**	WHAT IS
THE PART OF A TREE FROM WHICH QUININE & ASPIRIN'S SALICYLIC ACID ARE EXTRACTED	**$400**	WHAT IS
CROWBARS, NUTCRACKERS & ICE TONGS ARE DIFFERENT TYPES OF THIS SIMPLE MACHINE	**$600**	WHAT IS
THIS ORDER OF MAMMALS IS DIVIDED INTO PROSIMIANS & ANTHROPOIDS	**$800**	WHAT IS
IN A CHEMICAL PROCESS, MONOMERS, SMALL MOLECULES, LINK IN CHAINS TO FORM THESE LARGE MOLECULES	**$1000**	WHAT ARE

DOUBLE JEOPARDY!

SCIENCE

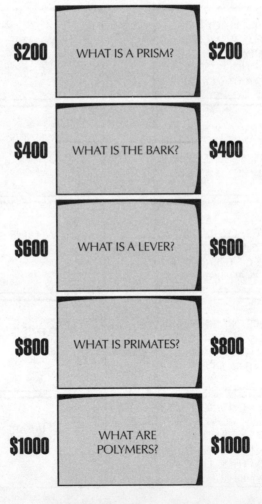

$200 WHAT IS A PRISM? **$200**

$400 WHAT IS THE BARK? **$400**

$600 WHAT IS A LEVER? **$600**

$800 WHAT IS PRIMATES? **$800**

$1000 WHAT ARE POLYMERS? **$1000**

DOUBLE JEOPARDY!

CRYING

SHE WEPT IN 1998 WHEN PRESIDENT CLINTON AGREED TO SETTLE HER HARASS-MENT LAWSUIT	**$200**	WHO IS
AS JIM BAKKER'S WIFE, THIS TELEVANGELIST WAS KNOWN FOR PUTTING ON MASCARA & SHEDDING TEARS	**$400**	WHO IS
IN 1961 JIMMY STEWART WEPT WHILE ACCEPTING AN OSCAR FOR THIS TERMINALLY ILL "HIGH NOON" STAR	**$600**	WHO IS
HIS APPARENT TEARS DURING A NEW HAMP-SHIRE CAMPAIGN STOP DAMAGED HIS 1972 PRESIDENTIAL BID	**$800**	WHO IS
THE ANTI-POLLUTION COMMERCIAL IN WHICH AN INDIAN SHEDS ONE TEAR FEATURED ACTOR OSCAR CODY, NICK-NAMED THIS	**$1000**	WHAT IS

DOUBLE JEOPARDY!

CRYING

$200	WHO IS PAULA JONES?	**$200**
$400	WHO IS TAMMY FAYE BAKKER?	**$400**
$600	WHO IS GARY COOPER?	**$600**
$800	WHO IS EDMUND S. MUSKIE?	**$800**
$1000	WHAT IS IRON EYES?	**$1000**

FINAL JEOPARDY!

U.S. GEOLOGY

THIS 800-MILE-LONG
FEATURE WAS DISCOVERED
& NAMED BY
ANDREW LAWSON

WHAT IS

FINAL JEOPARDY!

U.S. GEOLOGY

WHAT IS THE
SAN ANDREAS FAULT?

JEOPARDY!™

CREEPERS & CRAWLERS

THE WORMLIKE LARVA OF A BUTTERFLY OR MOTH	**$100**	WHAT IS
WHEN REFERRING TO THE GLASS LIZARD, AUTOTOMY IS THE ABILITY TO DISCARD ALL OR PART OF THIS	**$200**	WHAT IS
THIS DARK LADY, LATRODECTUS MACTANS, EARNS HER MORE COMMON NAME BY KILLING & EATING HER MATE	**$300**	WHAT IS
THESE NOISEMAKERS CAN BE SIDEWINDERS OR DIAMONDBACKS	**$400**	WHAT ARE
FOUND ON INDONESIAN ISLANDS, THESE MONITORS ARE THE WORLD'S LARGEST LIVING LIZARDS	**$500**	WHAT ARE

JEOPARDY!

CREEPERS & CRAWLERS

$100	WHAT IS A CATERPILLAR?	**$100**
$200	WHAT IS THE TAIL?	**$200**
$300	WHAT IS THE BLACK WIDOW?	**$300**
$400	WHAT ARE RATTLESNAKES?	**$400**
$500	WHAT ARE KOMODO DRAGONS?	**$500**

JEOPARDY!

U.S. MUSEUMS

WHEN DRIVING THROUGH SOUTH BEND IN THIS STATE, YOU CAN VISIT THE STUDEBAKER NATIONAL MUSEUM	**$100**	WHAT IS
WHEN YOU CARE ENOUGH TO VISIT THE VERY BEST, STOP BY THIS COMPANY'S VISITORS CENTER & MUSEUM IN KANSAS CITY	**$200**	WHAT IS
THIS CONFEDERATE TRAIN STOLEN DURING THE CIVIL WAR IS HOUSED AT GEORGIA'S BIG SHANTY MUSEUM	**$300**	WHAT IS
THE BUFFALO BILL MUSEUM IN THIS SMALL WYOMING CITY ALSO DISPLAYS ANNIE OAKLEY'S POSSESSIONS	**$400**	WHAT IS
ELIE WIESEL HELPED LIGHT AN ETERNAL FLAME AT THE 1993 DEDICATION OF THIS WASHINGTON, D.C. MUSEUM	**$500**	WHAT IS

JEOPARDY!

U.S. MUSEUMS

$100 | WHAT IS INDIANA? | $100

$200 | WHAT IS HALLMARK? | $200

$300 | WHAT IS THE GENERAL? | $300

$400 | WHAT IS CODY? | $400

$500 | WHAT IS THE HOLOCAUST MEMORIAL MUSEUM? | $500

JEOPARDY!

"BIG" STUFF

IT THEORETICALLY HAPPENED ABOUT 10 TO 20 BILLION YEARS AGO	**$100**	WHAT IS
A MAN WITH MORE THAN ONE CURRENT MOTHER-IN-LAW	**$200**	WHAT IS
THIS HARDY SHEEP SHARES ITS NAME WITH A RIVER & A MOUNTAIN RANGE	**$300**	WHAT IS
GEORGE ORWELL'S OPPRESSIVE "SIBLING"	**$400**	WHO IS
A 1930 WALLACE BEERY MOVIE, OR SLANG FOR A PENITENTIARY	**$500**	WHAT IS

JEOPARDY!

"BIG" STUFF

$100   WHAT IS THE BIG BANG? $100

$200   WHAT IS A BIGAMIST? $200

$300   WHAT IS THE BIGHORN? $300

$400   WHO IS BIG BROTHER? $400

$500   WHAT IS THE BIG HOUSE? $500

JEOPARDY!

MOVIE QUOTES

1931 CHILLER THAT FEATURES "IT'S ALIVE! IT'S ALIVE!"	**$100**	WHAT IS
TITLE CHARACTER WHO SAYS, "PAY NO ATTENTION TO THAT MAN BEHIND THE CURTAIN"	**$200**	WHO IS
IN A 1967 FILM THIS ACTOR STERNLY INFORMS US THAT "THEY CALL ME MR. TIBBS!"	**$300**	WHO IS
IN "THE GRADUATE", "I JUST WANT TO SAY ONE WORD TO YOU— JUST ONE WORD . . ." THIS	**$400**	WHAT IS
DE NIRO-GRODIN PICTURE WITH THE MEMORABLE LINE "OF COURSE THEY'RE GAINING ON US! THEY'RE FLYING!"	**$500**	WHAT IS

JEOPARDY!

MOVIE QUOTES

$100	WHAT IS "FRANKENSTEIN"?	$100
$200	WHO IS THE WIZARD OF OZ?	$200
$300	WHO IS SIDNEY POITIER?	$300
$400	WHAT IS "PLASTICS"?	$400
$500	WHAT IS "MIDNIGHT RUN"?	$500

242

JEOPARDY!

KINGS & QUEENS

THIS BIBLICAL KING DID A BAD BAD THING WHEN HE IMPREGNATED BATHSHEBA	**$100**	WHO IS
OF THE 6 BRITISH KINGS WHO BORE THIS NAME, THE FIRST 4 WERE OF THE GERMAN HOUSE OF HANOVER	**$200**	WHAT IS
ABDULLAH BECAME KING OF THIS COUNTRY IN 1999, SUCCEEDING HIS FATHER, HUSSEIN	**$300**	WHAT IS
THIS HAWAIIAN KING WHOSE NAME MEANS "THE VERY LONELY ONE" CONQUERED MAUI IN 1790	**$400**	WHO IS
THIS KING OF CASTILE & ARAGON WAS KNOWN AS "THE CATHOLIC"	**$500**	WHO IS

JEOPARDY!

KINGS & QUEENS

$100	WHO IS KING DAVID?	**$100**
$200	WHAT IS GEORGE?	**$200**
$300	WHAT IS JORDAN?	**$300**
$400	WHO IS KAMEHAMEHA?	**$400**
$500	WHO IS FERDINAND (II OR V)?	**$500**

JEOPARDY!

IVANS

Clue	Value	Response
IN THIS DOSTOYEVSKY NOVEL, IVAN IS THE ATHEISTIC INTELLECTUAL OF THE 4 SONS	$100	WHAT IS
IVAN WAS THE MIDDLE NAME OF THIS ASTRONAUT, VIRGIL WAS HIS FIRST, BUT MOST PEOPLE CALLED HIM "GUS"	$200	WHO IS
AS DIRECTOR OF "TWINS" & "KINDERGARTEN COP", HE TOLD ARNOLD SCHWARZENEGGER WHAT TO DO	$300	WHO IS
IN A 1985 BOOK HE CALLED ARBITRAGE "WALL STREET'S BEST KEPT MONEY-MAKING SECRET"	$400	WHO IS
HE MUST HAVE SALIVATED OVER HIS JOB TEACHING PHYSIOLOGY AT THE INSTITUTE OF EXPERIMENTAL MEDICINE	$500	WHO IS

JEOPARDY!

IVANS

$100   WHAT IS "THE BROTHERS KARAMAZOV"? $100

$200   WHO IS GUS GRISSOM? $200

$300   WHO IS IVAN REITMAN? $300

$400   WHO IS IVAN BOESKY? $400

$500   WHO IS IVAN PAVLOV? $500

DOUBLE JEOPARDY!

PRESIDENTIAL NICKNAMES

SUCCEEDING "TRICKY DICK", HE WAS JUST PLAIN "JERRY"	**$200**	WHO IS
HE WAS "THE ATLAS OF AMERICA" AS WELL AS "FIRST IN WAR", ETC.	**$400**	WHO IS
"BIG BEN" WOULD HAVE BEEN NICE; EVEN "GENTLE BEN"; BUT NO, HE HAD TO BE "LITTLE BEN"	**$600**	WHO IS
THE 1844 ELECTION MADE HIM "THE FIRST DARK HORSE"	**$800**	WHO IS
THIS 19th CENTURY PRESIDENT MADE THE LADIES QUIVER AS "HANDSOME FRANK"	**$1000**	WHO IS

DOUBLE JEOPARDY!

PRESIDENTIAL NICKNAMES

$200 — WHO IS GERALD FORD? — $200

$400 — WHO IS GEORGE WASHINGTON? — $400

$600 — WHO IS BENJAMIN HARRISON? — $600

$800 — WHO IS JAMES K. POLK? — $800

$1000 — WHO IS FRANKLIN PIERCE? — $1000

DOUBLE JEOPARDY!

LATIN

CITIUS, ALTIUS, FORTIUS—SWIFTER, HIGHER, STRONGER— IS THE MOTTO OF THIS EVENT	**$200**	WHAT ARE
USED AS A FOOTNOTE ABBREVIATION, THIS WORD MEANS "IN THE SAME PLACE"	**$400**	WHAT IS
DESCARTES' "JE PENSE, DONC JE SUIS" IS BETTER KNOWN AS THIS LATIN PHRASE	**$600**	WHAT IS
IT'S THE ENGLISH TRANSLATION OF "ARS GRATIA ARTIS", THE MOTTO OF MGM	**$800**	WHAT IS
IN "THE SILENCE OF THE LAMBS" HANNIBAL LECTER BARGAINS WITH CLARICE USING THIS PHRASE MEANING "WHAT FOR WHAT"	**$1000**	WHAT IS

DOUBLE JEOPARDY!

LATIN

$200 — WHAT ARE THE OLYMPIC GAMES? — $200

$400 — WHAT IS IBID(EM)? — $400

$600 — WHAT IS COGITO ERGO SUM? — $600

$800 — WHAT IS "ART FOR ART'S SAKE"? — $800

$1000 — WHAT IS QUID PRO QUO? — $1000

DOUBLE JEOPARDY!

POP MUSIC

AMONG THE THEMES HE COMPOSED FOR BLAKE EDWARDS WERE "PETER GUNN" & "THE PINK PANTHER"	**$200**	WHO IS
HIS BACKUP BAND IS THE BUCKAROOS	**$400**	WHO IS
THE 1998 ALBUM "PAINTED FROM MEMORY" PAIRED THIS COMPOSER & ELVIS COSTELLO	**$600**	WHO IS
SHE COVERED "(I CAN'T GET NO) SATISFACTION" ON HER ALBUM "OOPS! . . . I DID IT AGAIN"	**$800**	WHO IS
VERONICA BENNETT FRONTED THIS "BE MY BABY" GROUP	**$1000**	WHAT IS

DOUBLE JEOPARDY!

POP MUSIC

$200 WHO IS HENRY MANCINI? $200

$400 WHO IS BUCK OWENS? $400

$600 WHO IS BURT BACHARACH? $600

$800 WHO IS BRITNEY SPEARS? $800

$1000 WHAT IS THE RONETTES? $1000

DOUBLE JEOPARDY!

ICELAND COMETH

Clue	Value	Response
LOCATED ON FAXA BAY, IT WAS MADE THE CAPITAL OF ICELAND IN 1918	**$200**	WHAT IS
ICELAND'S NEAREST NEIGHBOR IS THIS ISLAND, ABOUT 190 MILES TO THE NORTHWEST	**$400**	WHAT IS
ICELAND WAS THE SITE OF ARMS CONTROL TALKS BETWEEN THESE 2 WORLD LEADERS IN OCTOBER 1986	**$600**	WHO ARE
96% OF THE POP-ULATION IS AFFILIATED WITH THE CHURCH OF ICELAND, WHICH IS THE EVANGELICAL TYPE OF THIS RELIGION	**$800**	WHAT IS
IN 1944 ICELAND GAINED FULL INDEPENDENCE FROM THIS PENINSULAR EUROPEAN COUNTRY	**$1000**	WHAT IS

DOUBLE JEOPARDY!

ICELAND COMETH

$200	WHAT IS REYKJAVIK?	**$200**
$400	WHAT IS GREENLAND?	**$400**
$600	WHO ARE RONALD REAGAN & MIKHAIL GORBACHEV?	**$600**
$800	WHAT IS LUTHERAN?	**$800**
$1000	WHAT IS DENMARK?	**$1000**

DOUBLE JEOPARDY!

BETTER MOUSETRAPS

THIS SWIMSUIT MADE ITS DEBUT SHORTLY AFTER THE APPEARANCE OF A MUSHROOM CLOUD OVER THIS PACIFIC ATOLL	**$200**	WHAT IS
KEEP YOUR COFFEE WARM IN ONE OF THESE BOTTLES INVENTED BY SIR JAMES DEWAR IN 1892	**$400**	WHAT IS
ARTHUR FRY DEVELOPED THIS PRODUCT FOR 3M AFTER TRYING TO BETTER MARK PAGES IN HIS HYMNAL	**$600**	WHAT ARE
SURE HOPE THIS GUY DIDN'T "BLIMP" UP WHILE CELEBRATING HIS INVENTION OF VULCANIZED RUBBER	**$800**	WHO IS
THIS BLACKSMITH IMPROVED THE PLOW IN THE LATE 1830s BY BUILDING THE FIRST ONE OF STEEL	**$1000**	WHO IS

DOUBLE JEOPARDY!

BETTER MOUSETRAPS

$200 — WHAT IS BIKINI? — $200

$400 — WHAT IS A THERMOS? — $400

$600 — WHAT ARE POST-IT NOTES? — $600

$800 — WHO IS CHARLES GOODYEAR? — $800

$1000 — WHO IS JOHN DEERE? — $1000

DOUBLE JEOPARDY!

NAMES WE KNOW

THE LEADER OF ROCK & ROLL'S FAMILY STONE	**$200**	WHO IS
THIS 18-YEAR-OLD, A HERO IN THE FIGHT AGAINST AIDS, DIED IN INDIANA IN APRIL 1990	**$400**	WHO IS
THIS BRILLIANT ACTRESS, OSCAR-NOMINATED FOR "BEING JOHN MALKOVICH", IS MARRIED TO ACTOR DERMOT MULRONEY	**$600**	WHO IS
MUCH PHOTOGRAPHED IN 2000, MARISLEYSIS IS THE COUSIN OF THIS FAMOUS LITTLE CUBAN	**$800**	WHO IS
THIS FORMER HEAD OF THE URBAN LEAGUE & OF BILL CLINTON'S TRANSITION TEAM TESTIFIED ON TAPE FEB. 2, 1999	**$1000**	WHO IS

DOUBLE JEOPARDY!

NAMES WE KNOW

$200 — WHO IS SLY (STONE)? — $200

$400 — WHO IS RYAN WHITE? — $400

$600 — WHO IS CATHERINE KEENER? — $600

$800 — WHO IS ELIAN GONZALEZ? — $800

$1000 — WHO IS VERNON JORDAN (JR.)? — $1000

FINAL JEOPARDY!

ENTERTAINMENT AWARDS

IN 1998 SHE BECAME
THE FIRST WOMAN
TO WIN AN OSCAR &
AN EMMY FOR LEAD
ACTRESS IN THE SAME YEAR

WHO IS

FINAL JEOPARDY!

ENTERTAINMENT AWARDS

WHO IS HELEN HUNT?

JEOPARDY!

FAMOUS NAMES

Clue	Value	Response
"LITTLE RED RIDING HOOD", A FILM HE ANIMATED IN 1922, WAS FOUND IN LONDON AROUND 20 YEARS AGO	$100	WHO IS
FAMOUS NICKNAME OF JOHN BIRKS GILLESPIE	$200	WHAT IS
THIS FAMOUS U-2 RECONNAISSANCE PILOT LATER BECAME A HELICOPTER TRAFFIC REPORTER	$300	WHO IS
THIS CARTOONIST FAMOUS FOR HIS "FAMILY" PUBLISHED "DRAWN AND QUARTERED" IN 1942	$400	WHO IS
HE SURPRISED MANY BY WITHDRAWING FROM THE 2000 NEW YORK SENATE RACE FOR PERSONAL REASONS	$500	WHO IS

JEOPARDY!

FAMOUS NAMES

$100   WHO IS WALT DISNEY? $100

$200   WHAT IS DIZZY? $200

$300   WHO IS FRANCIS GARY POWERS? $300

$400   WHO IS CHARLES ADDAMS? $400

$500   WHO IS RUDOLPH GIULIANI? $500

JEOPARDY!

U.S. HISTORY

THE HOSTAGES HELD IN THIS COUNTRY WERE FREED MOMENTS AFTER REAGAN'S 1981 INAUGURATION	**$100**	WHAT IS
HER FIRST ATTEMPT TO FLY AROUND THE WORLD ENDED IN MARCH 1937 WHEN HER PLANE CRASHED IN HAWAII	**$200**	WHO IS
SAMUEL GOMPERS HELPED FOUND THE AMERICAN FEDER-ATION OF THIS	**$300**	WHAT IS
RUGGED-SOUNDING GROUP THAT STORMED SAN JUAN HILL ON JULY 1, 1898	**$400**	WHO ARE
IN 1952 CONGRESS APPROVED THIS COMMONWEALTH'S NEW CONSTITUTION	**$500**	WHAT IS

JEOPARDY!

U.S. HISTORY

$100	WHAT IS IRAN?	$100
$200	WHO IS AMELIA EARHART?	$200
$300	WHAT IS LABOR?	$300
$400	WHO ARE THE ROUGH RIDERS?	$400
$500	WHAT IS PUERTO RICO?	$500

JEOPARDY!

NONPOTENT POTABLES

IN 1990 COCA-COLA INTRODUCED POWERADE TO COMPETE WITH THIS NO. 1-SELLING SPORTS DRINK	**$100**	WHAT IS
UNDER ITS MUG BRAND, PEPSICO MARKETS ROOT BEER & THIS DRINK FLAVORED WITH VANILLA	**$200**	WHAT IS
IN THE 1920s NATALI OLIVIERI HAD THE BRILLIANT IDEA OF FLAVORING YOO-HOO POP WITH THIS SWEET	**$300**	WHAT IS
THIS NORTHWEST CITY WAS A COFFEE MECCA PRE-WWII, LONG BEFORE STARBUCKS BEGAN THERE IN 1971	**$400**	WHAT IS
THIS SPARKLING LIQUID NAMED FOR A GERMAN TOWN WAS A FORE-RUNNER OF SODA POP	**$500**	WHAT IS

JEOPARDY!

NONPOTENT POTABLES

$100	WHAT IS GATORADE?	**$100**
$200	WHAT IS CREAM SODA?	**$200**
$300	WHAT IS CHOCOLATE?	**$300**
$400	WHAT IS SEATTLE?	**$400**
$500	WHAT IS SELTZER (WATER)?	**$500**

JEOPARDY!™

"G" WHIZ!

IT'S A MERE STRIP OF GARMENT WORN BY STRIPPERS	**$100**	WHAT IS
IT'S THE CAUTIOUS WAY ASTAIRE MIGHT HAVE HELD ROGERS IF SHE WAS IN A BAD MOOD	**$200**	WHAT IS
IN THE EARLY '70s TITLEIST ENGINEERS DEVELOPED THE ICOSAHEDRON DIMPLE PATTERN FOR THESE	**$300**	WHAT ARE
TO "STRAIN AT" THIS INSECT "AND SWALLOW A CAMEL" MEANS TO FUSS OVER TRIFLES BUT IGNORE SERIOUS PROBLEMS	**$400**	WHAT IS
A PROFESSIONAL ERRAND-RUNNER, WHETHER OR NOT HE HAS CHEEK POUCHES	**$500**	WHAT IS

267

JEOPARDY!

"G" WHIZ!

$100	WHAT IS A G-STRING?	**$100**
$200	WHAT IS GINGERLY?	**$200**
$300	WHAT ARE GOLF BALLS?	**$300**
$400	WHAT IS A GNAT?	**$400**
$500	WHAT IS A GOFER?	**$500**

JEOPARDY!

MASTERPIECES OF ART

GILBERT STUART'S UNFINISHED "ATHENAEUM HEAD" PORTRAIT OF THIS MAN APPEARS ON THE $1 BILL	**$100**	WHO IS
THIS SPANIARD'S "WEEPING WOMAN" IS THOUGHT TO BE MODELED ON HIS MISTRESS, DORA MAAR	**$200**	WHO IS
A FAMOUS 1793 PAINTING BY JACQUES-LOUIS DAVID DEPICTS THIS ASSASSINATED FRENCHMAN IN HIS BATHTUB	**$300**	WHO IS
HIS "YELLOW CHRIST" DATES FROM 1889, BEFORE HE LEFT FOR THE PAGAN SOUTH SEAS	**$400**	WHO IS
BORN IN 1599, THIS STUDENT OF RUBENS IS FAMOUS FOR HIS PORTRAIT OF MARCHESA ELENA GRIMALDI AS WELL AS OF KINGS	**$500**	WHO IS

JEOPARDY!™

MASTERPIECES OF ART

$100   WHO IS GEORGE WASHINGTON? $100

$200   WHO IS PABLO PICASSO? $200

$300   WHO IS JEAN PAUL MARAT? $300

$400   WHO IS PAUL GAUGUIN? $400

$500   WHO IS ANTHONY VAN DYCK? $500

JEOPARDY!

TV SHOWS

SUMMER OF 2000 HIT SET ON REMOTE PULAU TIGA	**$100**	WHAT IS
NANCY CARTWRIGHT IS OVER 30 YEARS OLDER THAN THIS ANIMATED SON OF MARGE SHE VOICES	**$200**	WHO IS
A MESSAGE LEFT ON THIS ACTOR'S MACHINE MIGHT SAY, "LOVED YOU AS JIM ROCKFORD!"	**$300**	WHO IS
IN 2000 THIS SHOW STARRING MS. BRENNEMAN TOOK ON THE CONTROVERSIAL ISSUE OF BABY-SHAKING	**$400**	WHAT IS
KEN HOWARD STARRED IN THIS SERIES ABOUT A WHITE BASKETBALL COACH AT A TOUGH INNER-CITY SCHOOL	**$500**	WHAT IS

JEOPARDY!

TV SHOWS

$100	WHAT IS "SURVIVOR"?	**$100**
$200	WHO IS BART SIMPSON?	**$200**
$300	WHO IS JAMES GARNER?	**$300**
$400	WHAT IS "JUDGING AMY"?	**$400**
$500	WHAT IS "THE WHITE SHADOW"?	**$500**

DOUBLE JEOPARDY!

HOW TRAGIC

SKIING MISHAPS CLAIMED THE LIVES OF MICHAEL KENNEDY & THIS ENTERTAINER-TURNED-CONGRESSMAN	**$200**	WHO IS
THOUGH NEARBY, THE CALIFORNIAN NEVER HEARD THIS LINER'S DISTRESS CALL IN 1912; ITS RADIO OPERATOR WAS OFF DUTY	**$400**	WHAT IS
THIS SINGER LEFT US NOT IN A JET PLANE BUT IN A SMALL EXPERIMENTAL PLANE IN 1997	**$600**	WHO IS
THIS MAY 6, 1937 DISASTER WAS BROADCAST ON RADIO	**$800**	WHAT IS
THIS WRITER & WIFE OF A FAMOUS AUTHOR DIED IN A FIRE AT A MENTAL HOSPITAL IN 1948	**$1000**	WHO IS

273

DOUBLE JEOPARDY!

HOW TRAGIC

$200	WHO IS SONNY BONO?	**$200**
$400	WHAT IS THE TITANIC?	**$400**
$600	WHO IS JOHN DENVER?	**$600**
$800	WHAT IS THE HINDENBURG CRASH?	**$800**
$1000	WHO IS ZELDA FITZGERALD?	**$1000**

DOUBLE JEOPARDY!

FICTIONAL CHARACTERS

GET TOO CLOSE TO THIS BELOVED FEMME & QUASIMODO JUST MIGHT RING YOUR BELL	**$200**	WHO IS
HE & HIS DOG WOLF WERE HUNTING SQUIRRELS IN THE CATSKILLS WHEN HE FELL ASLEEP	**$400**	WHO IS
LAST NAME OF SOAMES & IRENE, THE 2 PRINCIPAL CHARACTERS IN JOHN GALSWORTHY'S 3-NOVEL "SAGA"	**$600**	WHAT IS
ROXANE MARRIED CHRISTIAN DE NEUVILLETTE NOT KNOWING HIS LOVE LETTERS WERE WRITTEN BY THIS POET & SOLDIER	**$800**	WHO IS
IN THIS THACKERAY WORK, SIR PITT PROPOSES TO BECKY BUT SHE'S ALREADY SECRETLY MARRIED TO HIS SON RAWDON	**$1000**	WHAT IS

DOUBLE JEOPARDY!

FICTIONAL CHARACTERS

$200	WHO IS ESMERALDA?	$200
$400	WHO IS RIP VAN WINKLE?	$400
$600	WHAT IS FORSYTE?	$600
$800	WHO IS CYRANO DE BERGERAC?	$800
$1000	WHAT IS "VANITY FAIR"?	$1000

DOUBLE JEOPARDY!

KING CHARLES

A HOLIDAY IS NAMED FOR THIS BUILDING CHARLES V ADDED TO THE FORTIFICATIONS OF PARIS	$200	WHAT IS
ENGLAND'S CHARLES I DISMISSED IT IN 1629, RULED WITHOUT IT FOR 11 YEARS, THEN CALLED A SHORT ONE	$400	WHAT IS
HOLY ROMAN EMPEROR CHARLES II WAS NICKNAMED THIS; WE GUESS HE WASN'T THE HAIR APPARENT TO THE THRONE	$600	WHAT IS
THIS WOMAN WAS INSTRUMENTAL IN PUTTING THE DAUPHIN ON THE THRONE OF FRANCE AS KING CHARLES VII	$800	WHO IS
CHARLES III OF SPAIN MADE RELIGIOUS NEWS BY CURBING THIS INSTITUTION & EXPELLING THE JESUITS	$1000	WHAT IS

DOUBLE JEOPARDY!

KING CHARLES

$200   WHAT IS THE BASTILLE? $200

$400   WHAT IS PARLIAMENT? $400

$600   WHAT IS THE BALD? $600

$800   WHO IS JOAN OF ARC? $800

$1000   WHAT IS THE INQUISITION? $1000

DOUBLE JEOPARDY!

THE SHORT VERSION

Clue	Value	Response
IN A COURTROOM, IT'S WHAT D.A. STANDS FOR	$200	WHAT IS
IN A LETTER, THIS ABBREVIATION PRECEDES AN AFTERTHOUGHT	$400	WHAT IS
BMW IS SHORT FOR THIS CAR COMPANY	$600	WHAT IS
LASER IS AN ACRONYM FOR LIGHT AMPLIFICATION BY STIMULATED EMISSION OF THIS	$800	WHAT IS
IN MEDICINE, HIV STANDS FOR THIS	$1000	WHAT IS

DOUBLE JEOPARDY!
THE SHORT VERSION

$200 | WHAT IS DISTRICT ATTORNEY? | $200

$400 | WHAT IS P.S.? | $400

$600 | WHAT IS BAVARIAN MOTOR WORKS? | $600

$800 | WHAT IS RADIATION? | $800

$1000 | WHAT IS HUMAN IMMUNODEFICIENCY VIRUS? | $1000

DOUBLE JEOPARDY!

BRITISH ACTRESSES

IN 1998 CLAIRE FORLANI GOT TO "MEET" THIS TITLE CHARACTER PLAYED BY BRAD PITT	$200	WHO IS
"SENSE AND SENSIBILITY" STAR WHO HAD A LONG PERSONAL & PROFESSIONAL PARTNERSHIP WITH KENNETH BRANAGH	$400	WHO IS
HELENA BONHAM CARTER USED A YANK ACCENT TO PLAY THIS MAN'S WIFE IN "MIGHTY APHRODITE"	$600	WHO IS
IN THE LATE '70s SHE STARRED AS FONTAINE KHALED IN "THE STUD", BASED ON A NOVEL BY HER SISTER	$800	WHO IS
FIRST NAME OF NATASHA RICHARDSON'S SISTER, SEEN IN 2000 IN "THE PATRIOT"	$1000	WHAT IS

DOUBLE JEOPARDY!

BRITISH ACTRESSES

$200 — WHO IS JOE BLACK? — $200

$400 — WHO IS EMMA THOMPSON? — $400

$600 — WHO IS WOODY ALLEN? — $600

$800 — WHO IS JOAN COLLINS? — $800

$1000 — WHAT IS JOELY? — $1000

DOUBLE JEOPARDY!

ON THE ROAD

Clue	Value	Response
THE NATIONAL ARCHIVES EXHIBITION HALL IS ON THIS AVENUE, ALSO THE NAME OF A DOCUMENT HOUSED THERE	$200	WHAT IS
IT'S A MARTIN MILNER TV SHOW AS WELL AS A HISTORIC HIGHWAY	$400	WHAT IS
"THE STRIP", WHERE YOU'LL FIND CAESARS PALACE & THE MIRAGE, IS PROPERLY NAMED THIS BOULEVARD	$600	WHAT IS
YOU'LL FIND CLUBS LIKE THE WHISKY ON THE "STRIP" PART OF THIS L.A. BOULEVARD	$800	WHAT IS
THIS GLAMOROUS 1.18-MILE-LONG FRENCH STREET ENDING AT THE OBELISK OF LUXOR ALSO BOASTS A McDONALD'S	$1000	WHAT IS

DOUBLE JEOPARDY!

ON THE ROAD

$200	WHAT IS CONSTITUTION AVENUE?	**$200**
$400	WHAT IS ROUTE 66?	**$400**
$600	WHAT IS LAS VEGAS (BOULEVARD)?	**$600**
$800	WHAT IS SUNSET (BOULEVARD)?	**$800**
$1000	WHAT IS THE CHAMPS-ELYSEES?	**$1000**

FINAL JEOPARDY!

CABLE TV

SPAWNING A WEB SITE,
VIDEOS & A MAGAZINE, THIS
A&E SERIES ONCE HOSTED
BY PETER GRAVES TOOK ON
A LIFE OF ITS OWN

WHAT IS

FINAL JEOPARDY!
CABLE TV

WHAT IS
"BIOGRAPHY"?

JEOPARDY!

17th CENTURY AMERICA

IN 1609 THIS SETTLE-MENT HAD ABOUT 500 PEOPLE, BUT DISEASE & STARVATION CUT THE NUMBER TO 60 BY SPRING 1610	**$100**	WHAT IS
IN 1614 THIS HUSBAND OF POCAHONTAS SENT THE FIRST EXPORT CARGO OF TOBACCO TO ENGLAND	**$200**	WHO IS
IN 1635 THE PUBLIC LATIN SCHOOL, THE FIRST PUBLIC SCHOOL IN BRITISH AMERICA, WAS ESTABLISHED IN THIS CITY	**$300**	WHAT IS
ON JANUARY 5, 1665 THE NEW HAVEN COLONY WAS FOR-MALLY ANNEXED BY THIS COLONY	**$400**	WHAT IS
ON APRIL 9, 1682 THIS FRENCHMAN REACHED THE MOUTH OF THE MISSISSIPPI RIVER & CLAIMED THE REGION	**$500**	WHO IS

JEOPARDY!

17th CENTURY AMERICA

$100 — WHAT IS JAMESTOWN? — $100

$200 — WHO IS JOHN ROLFE? — $200

$300 — WHAT IS BOSTON? — $300

$400 — WHAT IS CONNECTICUT? — $400

$500 — WHO IS (SIEUR DE) LA SALLE? — $500

JEOPARDY!

AUTHORS

SAMUEL CLEMENS FIRST USED THIS PSEUDONYM ON FEBRUARY 3, 1863 IN VIRGINIA CITY'S TERRITORIAL ENTERPRISE	**$100**	WHAT IS
HIS "TROPIC OF CAPRICORN" WAS FIRST PUBLISHED IN FRANCE IN 1939; ITS U.S. RELEASE CAME 23 YEARS LATER	**$200**	WHO IS
IN 2000 HE WON AN OSCAR FOR ADAPTING HIS OWN NOVEL "THE CIDER HOUSE RULES"	**$300**	WHO IS
THE TOWN OF RED CLOUD, NEBRASKA HAS A HISTORICAL CENTER DEVOTED TO THIS AUTHOR	**$400**	WHO IS
IN 1999 THIS 84-YEAR-OLD AUTHOR OF "HUMBOLDT'S GIFT" & "MR. SAMMLER'S PLANET" BECAME A FATHER	**$500**	WHO IS

JEOPARDY!

AUTHORS

$100   WHAT IS
MARK TWAIN?   **$100**

$200   WHO IS
HENRY MILLER?   **$200**

$300   WHO IS
JOHN IRVING?   **$300**

$400   WHO IS
WILLA CATHER?   **$400**

$500   WHO IS
SAUL BELLOW?   **$500**

JEOPARDY!

BEAN COUNTING

TO MAKE THE POPULAR MEXICAN DISH FRIJOLES NEGROS, BEGIN WITH THESE BEANS	$100	WHAT ARE
IT'S THE BEAN WHOSE "MILK" IS USED TO MAKE TOFU	$200	WHAT IS
WHEN MAKING A HOMEMADE POT OF PORK & BEANS, YOU'LL BE AT SEA WITHOUT THESE BEANS	$300	WHAT ARE
LIKE CONTRACTS, RUNNER BEANS SHOULD HAVE NONE OF THESE ATTACHED; REMOVE THEM BEFORE COOKING	$400	WHAT ARE
THIS BEAN ENJOYED BY HANNIBAL LECTER IS ALSO KNOWN AS A BROAD BEAN	$500	WHAT IS

JEOPARDY!

BEAN COUNTING

$100	WHAT ARE BLACK BEANS?	$100
$200	WHAT IS THE SOY BEAN?	$200
$300	WHAT ARE NAVY BEANS?	$300
$400	WHAT ARE STRINGS?	$400
$500	WHAT IS A FAVA BEAN?	$500

JEOPARDY!

ON THE "DOUBLE"

TWINS ADVERTISE THIS FLAVOR OF WRIGLEY'S GUM	**$100**	WHAT IS
IT'S SLANG FOR THE OLD 55-MILE-PER-HOUR NATIONAL SPEED LIMIT	**$200**	WHAT IS
THE FIFTH AMEND-MENT PROTECTS AGAINST IT	**$300**	WHAT IS
A 1984 MELANIE GRIFFITH MOVIE, OR THE FUNCTION SHELLY MICHELLE SERVED FOR JULIA ROBERTS IN "PRETTY WOMAN"	**$400**	WHAT IS
"(JUST LIKE) STARTING OVER" IS ONE OF THE SONGS FROM THIS 1980 JOHN LENNON & YOKO ONO ALBUM	**$500**	WHAT IS

JEOPARDY!

ON THE "DOUBLE"

$100   WHAT IS DOUBLEMINT? $100

$200   WHAT IS THE DOUBLE NICKEL? $200

$300   WHAT IS DOUBLE JEOPARDY? $300

$400   WHAT IS A BODY DOUBLE? $400

$500   WHAT IS "DOUBLE FANTASY"? $500

JEOPARDY!

BRITISH POP

Clue	Value	Response
"2 BECOME 1" & "WANNABE" WERE SMASH HITS FOR THIS FEMALE QUINTET	$100	WHAT IS
"GOD SAVE THE QUEEN" IS A CLASSIC BY THIS PUNK ROCK BAND, THE LEADERS OF THE SECOND BRITISH INVASION	$200	WHAT IS
THE 2 DAVIES BROTHERS WERE THE CORE OF THIS BRITISH GROUP	$300	WHAT IS
THIS BAND'S "BITTER SWEET SYMPHONY" RECYCLED A ROLLING STONES RIFF	$400	WHAT IS
WITH "TELSTAR", THIS BAND NAMED FOR A WEATHER PHENOMENON WAS THE FIRST BRITISH GROUP TO TOP THE U.S. CHARTS	$500	WHAT IS

JEOPARDY!

BRITISH POP

$100	WHAT IS THE SPICE GIRLS? **$100**
$200	WHAT IS THE SEX PISTOLS? **$200**
$300	WHAT IS THE KINKS? **$300**
$400	WHAT IS THE VERVE? **$400**
$500	WHAT IS THE TORNADOES? **$500**

JEOPARDY!

PEOPLE & PLACES

A NEWCOMER TO THIS U.S. STATE IS KNOWN TO LOCALS AS A MALIHINI	**$100**	WHAT IS
PRESIDENTS OF TIBLISI & BATUMI, OR OF PLAINS & MACON	**$200**	WHAT ARE
A NATIVE OF FLANDERS, OR ICE SKATER PEGGY	**$300**	WHAT IS
BIGGER SWINGERS THAN MOST SOUTH AMERICANS, THE PEOPLE OF THIS CITY ARE CARAQUENOS	**$400**	WHAT IS
THE PEOPLE OF THIS BRITISH CITY ARE CALLED BRUMMIES, FROM BRUMMAGEM, AN OLD SLANG NAME FOR THE TOWN	**$500**	WHAT IS

JEOPARDY!™

PEOPLE & PLACES

$100	WHAT IS HAWAII?	$100
$200	WHAT ARE GEORGIANS?	$200
$300	WHAT IS A FLEMING?	$300
$400	WHAT IS CARACAS?	$400
$500	WHAT IS BIRMINGHAM?	$500

DOUBLE JEOPARDY!

SCIENCE & NATURE

THESE DARK PATCHES ON THE SUN'S SURFACE APPEAR & DISAPPEAR IN REGULAR CYCLES	**$200**	WHAT ARE
FROM THE GREEK FOR "YOKE", IT'S A CELL FORMED BY THE UNION OF 2 GAMETES	**$400**	WHAT IS
THIS "SEA" CREATURE IS A VASE-SHAPED POLYP WITH MOUTH SURROUNDED BY TENTACLES	**$600**	WHAT IS
SON OF A GUN! THIS FEMALE, SEED-BEARING PART OF A FLOWER CONSISTS OF A STIGMA, A STYLE & AN OVARY	**$800**	WHAT IS
ANNOUNCED ON FEBRUARY 14, 1946, THIS FIRST ELECTRONIC DIGITAL COMPUTER HAD 18,000 VACUUM TUBES	**$1000**	WHAT IS

299

DOUBLE JEOPARDY!

SCIENCE & NATURE

$200	WHAT ARE SUNSPOTS?	$200
$400	WHAT IS A ZYGOTE?	$400
$600	WHAT IS A SEA ANEMONE?	$600
$800	WHAT IS THE PISTIL?	$800
$1000	WHAT IS ENIAC?	$1000

DOUBLE JEOPARDY!

THAT'S HISTORY

FERDINAND & ISABELLA PROMISED TO MAKE HIM "ADMIRAL OF THE OCEAN SEA" IF HE WAS SUCCESSFUL IN HIS 1492 VOYAGE	**$200**	WHO IS
IN 1455 JOHANN FUST WON A JUDGMENT AGAINST THIS PRINTER & TOOK THE TYPE USED TO PRINT HIS FAMOUS BIBLE	**$400**	WHO IS
IN 1795 AUSTRIA, PRUSSIA & RUSSIA PARTITIONED THIS COUNTRY, ELIMINATING ITS EXISTENCE	**$600**	WHAT IS
AT THE DEATH OF CARDINAL MAZARIN IN 1661, THIS FRENCH KING DECLARED THAT HE WOULD SERVE AS HIS OWN PRIME MINISTER	**$800**	WHO IS
THIS ANCIENT NORTH AFRICAN CITY-STATE WAS PROTECTED BY A HIGH WALL ABOUT 23 MILES IN LENGTH	**$1000**	WHAT IS

DOUBLE JEOPARDY!

THAT'S HISTORY

$200	WHO IS CHRISTOPHER COLUMBUS?	**$200**
$400	WHO IS JOHANN(ES) GUTENBERG?	**$400**
$600	WHAT IS POLAND?	**$600**
$800	WHO IS LOUIS XIV?	**$800**
$1000	WHAT IS CARTHAGE?	**$1000**

DOUBLE JEOPARDY!

MUSKRAT LOVE

MUSKRAT FAMILIES OFTEN LIVE IN DENS CALLED THESE, LIKE THE HOMES OF BEAVERS & CERTAIN "ELKS"	$200	WHAT ARE
BECAUSE IT'S NATIVE TO THIS "SUNSHINE STATE", THE ROUND-TAILED MUSKRAT CAN BREED YEAR-ROUND	$400	WHAT IS
FROM LATIN FOR "BED", FEMALE MUSKRATS HAVE 2–5 OF THEM A YEAR WITH 5–7 YOUNG IN EACH	$600	WHAT IS
IN MUSKRATS THIS PERIOD, WHOSE NAME IS FROM LATIN FOR "CARRYING", LASTS LESS THAN A MONTH	$800	WHAT IS
IN BREEDING SEASON, 2 OF THESE ORGANS ENLARGE TO PRODUCE THE "MUSK" IN THE ANIMAL'S NAME	$1000	WHAT ARE

DOUBLE JEOPARDY!

MUSKRAT LOVE

$200 WHAT ARE LODGES? **$200**

$400 WHAT IS FLORIDA? **$400**

$600 WHAT IS A LITTER? **$600**

$800 WHAT IS GESTATION? **$800**

$1000 WHAT ARE GLANDS? **$1000**

DOUBLE JEOPARDY!

ORGANIZATIONS

IN 1997 THIS ORGANIZATION CELEBRATED THE 90th ANNIVERSARY OF ITS CHRISTMAS SEALS	**$200**	WHAT IS
AN ADORABLE LITTLE PANDA IS THE SYMBOL OF THIS "FUND" FOUNDED IN 1961	**$400**	WHAT IS
IN 1997 MARTIN LUTHER KING III WAS ELECTED PRESIDENT OF THIS GROUP, THE SCLC; DAD WOULD HAVE BEEN PROUD	**$600**	WHAT IS
THE "WORLD" ONE OF THESE IS OFFICIALLY THE "INTERNATIONAL" ONE "FOR RECONSTRUCTION & DEVELOPMENT"	**$800**	WHAT IS
AN ASSOCIATION IN ANNANDALE, VIRGINIA IS DEVOTED TO THIS MAN, JEFFERSON'S VICE PRESIDENT & THE SUBJECT OF A MILK AD	**$1000**	WHO IS

DOUBLE JEOPARDY!

ORGANIZATIONS

$200	WHAT IS THE AMERICAN LUNG ASSOCIATION?	$200
$400	WHAT IS THE WORLD WILDLIFE FUND?	$400
$600	WHAT IS THE SOUTHERN CHRISTIAN LEADERSHIP CONFERENCE?	$600
$800	WHAT IS BANK?	$800
$1000	WHO IS AARON BURR?	$1000

DOUBLE JEOPARDY!

TOUGH FOOTBALL

IN 1967 THIS NEW YORK JET BECAME THE FIRST NFL QUARTER-BACK TO THROW FOR OVER 4,000 YARDS IN A SEASON	**$200**	WHO IS
RUNNING BACK THURMAN THOMAS OF THIS TEAM IS THE ONLY PLAYER TO SCORE IN 4 CONSECUTIVE SUPER BOWLS	**$400**	WHAT ARE
HE TOOK OVER AS THE VIKINGS' COACH IN 1992 & LED THEM THROUGH THE REST OF THE '90s	**$600**	WHO IS
IN 1998 HIS 1,846 RUSHING YARDS HELPED THE ATLANTA FALCONS GET TO THE SUPER BOWL	**$800**	WHO IS
ON NOV. 8, 1970 THIS MAN HELPED THE SAINTS BEAT THE LIONS BY KICKING A RECORD-SETTING 63-YARD FIELD GOAL	**$1000**	WHO IS

DOUBLE JEOPARDY!

TOUGH FOOTBALL

$200 WHO IS JOE NAMATH? $200

$400 WHAT ARE
THE BUFFALO BILLS? $400

$600 WHO IS
DENNIS GREEN? $600

$800 WHO IS JAMAL
ANDERSON? $800

$1000 WHO IS
TOM DEMPSEY? $1000

DOUBLE JEOPARDY!

WRONG!

FOLLOW A FALSE LEAD & YOU'RE DOING THIS "UP THE WRONG TREE"	**$200**	WHAT IS
A BADLY MISTAKEN BASEBALL PLAYER IS WAY "OFF" THIS, BE IT FIRST OR HOME	**$400**	WHAT IS
"A CASE OF" THIS MAY INVOLVE PICKING THE WRONG PERSON OUT OF A POLICE LINE-UP	**$600**	WHAT IS
TIPO, ER . . . TYPO IS SHORT FOR THIS 2-WORD PHRASE	**$800**	WHAT IS
FRENCH FOR "FALSE STEP"; YOU DON'T WANT TO COMMIT A SOCIAL ONE	**$1000**	WHAT IS

DOUBLE JEOPARDY!

WRONG!

$200 — WHAT IS BARKING? — $200

$400 — WHAT IS BASE? — $400

$600 — WHAT IS MISTAKEN IDENTITY? — $600

$800 — WHAT IS TYPO-GRAPHICAL ERROR? — $800

$1000 — WHAT IS A FAUX PAS? — $1000

FINAL JEOPARDY!

COUNTRIES

THIS ISLAND NATION IS
THE ONLY COUNTRY IN
THE WORLD NAMED FOR
A BIBLICAL KING

WHAT ARE

FINAL JEOPARDY!

COUNTRIES

WHAT ARE THE
SOLOMON ISLANDS?